W9-AWU-317

This book is dedicated to all the police officers and
firefighters who lost their lives at the
World Trade Center on September 11, 2001.
It is also dedicated to all police officers around the
world who have paid the ultimate price
for upholding their sworn oath to protect
and serve, and to my best friend and
lifelong partner, my wife, Myong Cha.

I would like to thank my friends at Good News for
their assistance in putting this book together. Also, I
would like to thank New Fairfield United Methodist
Church for their continual love, prayer, and support.

CONTENTS

Beyond the Badge

Beyond the Badge

A Spiritual Survival Guide for Cops and Their Families

By Charles Ferrara
Lieutenant, NYPD (Ret.)

LIVING STREAMS PUBLICATIONS

Art direction and layout: Robert Rempfer
Cover design: Deltron Designs
Editor: Steve Beard
Assistant editor: Krista Hershey

First printed by Living Streams Publications, January 2006
Second printing, March 2006
Third printing, June 2006
Fourth printing, November 2006
Fifth printing, March 2007
Sixth printing, May 2007
Seventh printing, March 2008
Eighth printing, February 2011
Ninth printing, August 2016

Living Streams Publications is a ministry of Good News, a renewal movement within the United Methodist Church.

For more information, contact:
Good News
P.O. Box 132076
The Woodlands, TX 77393-2076
(832) 813-8327

A day that will never be forgotten

On September 11, 2001, members of the Al Quaida terrorist network flew two commercial jets into the World Trade Center. On that sunny morning, New York City and the nation experienced their greatest tragedy. Sixty-six law enforcement officers perished while rescuing civilians out of the two super structures.

There are close to 750,000 law enforcement officers in the United States serving in 18,000 separate agencies. In any given year 62,200 of them are assaulted. Over 15,000 officers have been killed in the line-of-duty since 1972. On average, a police officer dies in the line-of-duty every 57 hours. During the last ten years, our nation has averaged 156 police officers killed each year. Of the 18,000 agencies, the NYPD is the largest municipal agency with some 40,000 sworn officers serving in 76 precincts and other specialized units.

How many Americans are willing to run into harm's way when everyone else is fleeing from it? How many are willing to charge through a door already knowing there is an armed and crazed individual inside? I suspect on average, not many.

These heroes are called to make life-or-death decisions that are easily second-guessed by Monday morning politicians, community activists, and the media. Critical evaluations on police performance are an easy matter once the adrenaline has subsided and the incident from the night before has been reduced to a Duty Captain's report. What does an officer do in a split second, when a car's occupant bolts from the passenger side of a stopped vehicle with an object in his hand? Is it a weapon? Is it a can of beer? The decision made on that dark street—shoot or don't shoot—can make the difference between a department trial and an inspector's funeral—from receiving formal charges or receiving the Medal of Honor. This book was written to cops from the heart and experiences of a former New York City cop in an effort to better help them survive what very few are ever called to do.

Looking Back
from Ground Zero

"It is not the critic who counts; not the man who points out how the strong man stumbled, or where a doer of deeds could have done them better. The credit belongs to the man who is actually in the arena; whose face is marred by dust and sweat and blood; who strives valiantly; who errs and comes short again and again; who knows the great enthusiasms, the great devotions, and spends himself in a worthy cause; who, at the best, knows in the end the triumph of high achievement; and who, at the worst, if he fails, at least fails while daring greatly, so that his place shall never be with those cold and timid souls who know neither victory nor defeat."

—*Theodore Roosevelt*
Former Police Commissioner, NYPD

I could have been an astronaut standing on the dusty surface of the moon, but it was actually the most expensive piece of real estate in the entire world. My feet rested on the powdery top landing of a subway entrance in the Wall Street District of New York City. People were walking around with surgical masks over their noses and mouths. There was a haze of smoke and white dust in the air with a beam of sunlight running through that gave me the impression I had entered heaven, but the surroundings and expressions on the faces of the people made it look more like I was about to enter hell.

As I made my way through National Guard and police checkpoints displaying my retired NYPD identification card, it wasn't long before I stood at the base of a huge pile of debris that once made up the two great towers of the World Trade Center. I knew this place like the back of my hand. I had worked its streets as a cop and supervisor. But I could not recognize the subtlest sign of the picture I had etched in my brain of what it should have looked like. I kept thinking this could not be the site of the World Trade Center. What inhumane act of terror could justify what I was looking at? It was as if Armageddon had begun—and its starting place was not in the Megiddo Valley in Israel, but on the southern tip of the Island of

7

Manhattan.

Firefighters and police officers were walking around in a daze suffering from shock, grief, and sleep depravation. "Hi Father," one fatigued firefighter said to me with a glance in my direction. I had almost forgotten that I was wearing a black clerical shirt and white collar.

New York City is my beloved city. It is where four generations of my family grew up. It is where I played stickball, pitched pennies, and went to school. It is where my father was born, where I was born, and where my children were born. It is where I enlisted in the Army to serve my country during the Viet Nam conflict. It was on these streets I had the privilege of serving in the greatest police department in the world.

I had traveled down to Ground Zero in the hopes of doing something constructive—something to help this tragic situation that had struck our nation. Now that I was there, no longer watching it on CNN or CNBC, I stood on a battlefield where our President made a declaration of war against terrorism. I stood on a site that was so horrendous, yet it felt like holy ground at the same time. I couldn't help but wonder what I could possibly offer these guys in the form of hope and encouragement. I felt so ill-equipped, so inadequate for the task at hand. If I were a cop again, I could help dig, give directions, set up a temporary headquarters—everything a cop or emergency services worker instinctively does. But I was in a different place. I was a man of the cloth, a representative of God in the midst of what had every indication of godlessness.

Staring at what became known as "the pile" with a sense of grief, pain, rage, and helplessness running through me—I considered returning home, wondering what possible good could I lend to such an enormous disaster. In that moment, I was reminded of a verse from the Bible, "Therefore we do not lose heart. Though outwardly we are wasting away, yet inwardly we are being renewed day by day. For our light and momentary troubles are achieving for us an eternal glory that far outweighs them all. So we fix our eyes not on what is seen, but on what is unseen. For what is seen is temporary, but what is unseen is eternal" (2 Corinthians 4:16).

I was given a whole new sense of hope and purpose from that moment on. I felt called to be an extension of God's love to the men and women who were in such anguish. Leaving the site that night, after members of the Red Cross cleaned the dust from my shoes at a washing station, I looked back from Ground Zero at all the years that God kept his hand on me, perhaps for that very moment in time. Thus, the reason for my writing this book is to look back over the years of my life and police experiences to not only help recall my small part in the history of the NYPD, but to also encourage police officers, firefighters, Emergency Services workers, military personnel, and anyone else who cares about and loves such a noble group of heroes.

This book is not meant to report the best or most heroic work performed within the history of the NYPD, but rather to share the day-to-day experiences of a normal "A-House" cop and supervisor. Some of the stories may appear to be incredible—to the average person they are—but not to a New York cop. Lord only knows what still rests in the minds of thousands of veteran officers that have never been revealed. Only recently have I shared some of my stories with family and close acquaintances. For decades they remained hidden away in the recesses of my mind, heart, and soul.

Before becoming a minister, I spent over fifteen years with the New York City Police Department, eventually retiring as a lieutenant while on the captain's promotion list. With the exception of my academy training and my last year as the Personnel Lieutenant with the Patrol Borough Manhattan South Command, all of my service time was as a street cop in high crime areas of the city. There are literally hundreds of stories floating around in my head and written on my heart—some of which I am extremely proud and others I'd rather forget.

During my time on the job, I met people of celebrity in the eyes of the public and some in their own minds. I worked with some of the best cops in the world—and others who should have never been given a badge and a gun. One thing I am certain of is that I love cops and respect the job they perform day in and day out. This book aims to make sense of not only what a cop is, but what it means to be a good one.

ONE

Welcome to the Two-Three, Kid

My first day in the precinct was an exciting one. My gig line was straight, shoes spit-shined, revolver clean and wedged in a holster that was so new and tight that if I needed my weapon it could never be drawn. I must have arrived at my first assignment in the 23rd Precinct two hours before my shift began. The 23rd Precinct was located in the tough part of Manhattan known as "Spanish Harlem" or "El Barrio." I remember reading every single post condition, alarm, or what some departments call a B.O.L.O. (be on the lookout) hanging on the bulletin board in the briefing room. All I did was write on the back pages of my memo book. I wrote down every stolen auto plate number, descriptions of wanted felons, or anything else that would help me capture my first bank robber.

Finally the hair bags, veteran officers, started filling up the room, pushing most of us rookies to the rear of the muster room. No one said hello or asked my name. They just joked around making fun of each other through war stories about some female known to everyone on East 102nd Street or how messed up the new contract was.

Just as we were about to receive our roll call assignments, a Hispanic man in his fifties entered the main area of the precinct with a machete in his hand—waving it around over his head like Teddy Roosevelt charging up San Juan Hill. I immediately reached for the butt of my weapon ready to draw it as instructed in the academy, but none of the senior officers even flinched. Without missing a beat, Sergeant Gilliam picked up a chair and cracked it over the man's head. The irate citizen crumbled to the floor like a deflated balloon. Still holding a clipboard in one hand, the sergeant ordered one of the officers to cuff the visitor and throw him in the holding cell. It was all over in a matter of seconds as the sergeant resumed reading off the names and assignments on the roll call sheet as if nothing unusual had happened. A seasoned officer named Gorman looked over at me

11

and said, "Welcome to the Two-three, kid."

I would like to believe that most police officers do not begin their careers as I did. However, earning the honor and privilege to wear the uniform of a police officer is something anyone should be proud of. Think of it—the city or county or state that has entrusted you to protect and serve has literally placed the lives of its citizens in your hands. That is an awesome responsibility. Other than a combat soldier, I cannot think of another profession that places its members in the authoritative position of holding the very balance of life and death in their hands. Paramedics, medical personnel, and fire fighters save lives—and so do police officers; the only difference is, everyday cops in our nation are placed in a position with the possibility of having to take a life—or losing their own.

I eventually settled in quite well in the two-three. Little by little the other officers realized I could carry my weight and be trusted to make good and quick decisions. One hot August night in Spanish Harlem, I was working Sector Eddie with an officer named Martinez. He wasn't my regular partner, but I was assigned with him because his partner took the night off. It wasn't often that a rookie was given a chance to ride in a sector car. Rookies were usually relegated to foot posts, special conditions, guarding prisoners at Metropolitan Hospital, or sitting with a D.O.A. But that night I was in a radio car and it felt good.

After answering a number of calls for service, there was a welcomed lull when the two of us could just rest for a moment and catch up with our paper work. Then the radio cracked with the dispatcher informing us that a band of teens just robbed a security guard at gunpoint. Racing to the scene we immediately spotted the wolf pack of youth running through a schoolyard alleyway. Martinez dropped me off at one end of the alley while he drove around to the other side to hopefully cut them off. I was a young officer at the time and had pretty good speed in a foot chase. In spite of what felt like a hundred pounds of equipment around my waist, I was off and running.

As I entered the darkened alleyway and started to close the gap between myself and the suspects, one of them turned and pulled a 9mm semi-automatic handgun from his waistband. In his attempt to fire a round at me, his gun discharged into the sidewalk, almost hitting his foot. The shock of the report of the weapon must have scared the heck out of him. He fumbled the weapon like a wide receiver boggling a football in the end zone. Never losing his stride of escape, his weapon fell to the ground. Bypassing the weapon, I continued the foot chase. The four young men beat my partner to the other end of the alley and ran across 5th Avenue and over the wall leading into Central Park—a virtual no man's land after sundown.

Dumping the radio car on 5th Avenue, Martinez and I entered the darkened park. Like a reconnaissance patrol seeking the enemy, we lowered the volume on our portable radios and slowly and systematically moved deeper into the park while allowing our night vision to adjust. About two minutes into our search we heard the scream of a female. Then we heard the sound of what appeared to be a slap or a punch of flesh hitting flesh. Another scream was partially muffled presumably by a person's hand over her mouth. As we moved in the direction of the cries for help, while looking for four armed robbers, we stumbled on a rape in progress and made the arrest.

My partner secured the rapist in the rear of our patrol car and paramedics cared for the rape victim. I ran back to the school alleyway and recovered the fully loaded 9mm Reuger handgun that could have very likely taken my life 20 minutes earlier. And to think—this was before bulletproof vests.

During the arraignment of my prisoner in Manhattan Criminal Court (who was eventually indicted and convicted of the charges of assault and rape) my lovely wife gave birth to our first child—a baby girl. I was a brand new dad, but the thought remained with me for years that my wife could have been a widow that night, and my daughter made fatherless before she even entered the world. Welcome to the two-three, kid.

TWO

What's a Good Cop?

What comes to the average person's mind when the term "cop" or "police officer" is invoked? Dirty Harry perhaps? Maybe one of the *Police Academy* movies or an episode of *NYPD Blue* comes into focus. In an attempt to place a face with the term cop, perhaps the likes of Bruce Willis or Jimmy Smits takes shape in the inner mind. The image of a cop is usually shaped in the mythic form of a Hollywood character or some negative portrayal given by the news media. But a cop is rarely, if ever, described as a "normal" person like you and me—a guy or gal who struggles to pay a mortgage, goes to church, mows a lawn, roots at his or her kid's little league game, and even occasionally hurts inside. Why is it so hard to erase that stereotypical macho image perpetrated over the years by Hollywood screenwriters?

There is a certain mystique about the workings of law enforcement. The thought of solving a big case, pursuing a serial killer, or engaging in a wild chase through the streets of some metropolis has captured the minds of kids for decades. Since I was knee-high, I was attracted to police officers and police work. My family informs me that I wanted to be a police officer ever since I could formulate thoughts into words.

I'll never forget when I was in elementary school, my fifth grade sidekick, Barry Farber, and I would carry our AAA school crossing guard badges with our Sergeant Joe Friday *Dragnet* I.D. cards and plastic snub-nosed revolvers and search for imaginary desperados in back alleys, hallways, and on the rooftops of buildings in Williamsburgh, Brooklyn. When most young boys hung out at fire houses gazing up at the big red fire trucks, I could be found sitting beneath the green light inscribed with the 92nd Precinct and observing everything the patrolmen did. I carefully watched how they escorted prisoners to the front desk, stood at attention for inspection by the sergeant and raced in and out of the block either returning from or responding to some

15

kind of emergency somewhere that only they knew through that neat gadget they had mounted in their radio car. Back then and still today an NYPD police cruiser is called an R.M.P. (Radio Motor Patrol) car. Today we use fiber optic, computer generated, hi-tech communications where officers can not only run a car registration, but actually have a person's criminal record returned in a matter of minutes.

I remember as a kid sending a letter to J. Edgar Hoover, then the director of the Federal Bureau of Investigation, requesting information about his agency. I explained in my letter how I would one day grow up and be a crime fighter. To my surprise, Mr. Hoover sent me a personally signed letter along with brochures about his elite bureau of investigators and a half dozen "wanted" posters of some of the most infamous criminals like Machine Gun Kelly, John Dillinger, and Al Capone.

To me, a cop was a real working person who lived next door and not some fictional character played by actors. I guess the real question for me is not "What's a cop?" but rather, "What's a good cop?" What does it mean to be a good cop? When I was on the job with the NYPD, it was common to hear police officers say, "So-and-so is a good cop." Usually it meant he made lots of collars (arrests) and could handle himself on the street—in other words, a tough cop.

Not too long ago I did something I rarely ever do—I watched a cop movie on cable television entitled, of all things, "Tough Cop," based on the book written by former New York City detective and frequent guest of the Don Imus radio show, Bo Dietel. I remember Bo as being a tough cop—or was he? Sure, he was able to handle himself on the street and knew all the ins and outs of the precinct he worked. But based on what I observed in the movie, he was a caring police officer who felt all of the emotions everyone else feels—pain, sadness, joy, anger, love, and disappointment. Does being a good or tough cop mean that the officer is void of all emotions and feelings?

To me, a good cop is a police officer who does the right thing. "Do the right thing" is another common phrase used by the members of the NYPD. "Hey kid," you would hear an older officer say, "Do the right thing." Since I have become a clergyman, this phrase takes on a different meaning for me. For obvious reasons, doing the right thing now means that I try to live righteously before God.

THREE

Everyone Needs a Guardian Angel

Many police officers have been given religious medals of St. Michael, the patron saint and Guardian Angel of Police Officers, by persons who love them. Well, St. Michael was on duty one particular night while I was working in Harlem.

It was a normal night patrolling the hot steamy streets of Harlem where everybody and his brother was out on the street, having felt how unbearably hot it was inside of the apartments. Standing on 8th Avenue in the area of West 118th Street, everything appeared to be quiet—quiet that is, for Harlem. I was chewing the fat with my partner, Dominic, when a scream for help broke the normal rhythm of sound waves crisscrossing our space.

"Help!" a woman screamed in desperation. "Help! They just took my bag!" Out of the corner of my eye I caught the fluid stride of two men running diagonally across the avenue away from where we were standing. No doubt it was two heroin users crazed in their minds and craving in their bodies for a fix. Nothing or no one would get in the way of their next score.

Thank goodness that during most of my police career I was in great shape. Serving as an officer in an Army Reserve Special Forces Group certainly kept me motivated to run five miles every day with weights on my ankles and a rucksack on my back. Like a shot out of a cannon, my partner and I took off after them while Dom called into central that we were in a foot pursuit of two males wanted for a bag snatch. Being street smart and having done this before, the two fleeing suspects split up in two directions, leaving me to pursue the guy with the bag and my partner to go after his accomplice. All that kept running through my mind was that I was going to get this guy. I

17

didn't take drugs, I rarely had a drink, I ate right, and worked out—this guy was a junkie, and I was going to take him down. The more this thought kept running through my head, the faster his pace became. It is strange what goes through your head during times like that.

I kept rationalizing that I had a belt of equipment around my waist weighing a ton. I was holding my hat in one hand and a portable radio in the other. I was wearing boots while he had on sneakers. But he was gaining and that ticked me off all the more. So I dug really deep inside with the best airborne finish a paratrooper could muster and began to close the gap as he looked back like a scared gazelle on *Wild Kingdom* being pursued by a lion.

Realizing I wasn't a donut-eating cop who was going to slow down or give up, he darted into an abandoned building that I knew to be occupied by squatters who used it as a shooting gallery and flop house. Whenever cops entered this building, people would run in all directions knowing "The Man" was in the house. Heroin addicts would limp along the hallways with ulcerated legs from shooting heroin in them because veins everywhere else had collapsed. Strange, but I always felt sorry for addicts. They were living in hell waiting to die, and it was only a matter of time. The thing I could never figure out was why the city allowed these buildings to exist. They had electricity and natural gas. So in the winter the junkies would huddle around a stove with all four burners going to heat the room. Who paid the electric and gas bills? No one ever could explain that one to me.

As I entered the hallway I could hear my prey's footsteps laboring up the marble steps of this once nice abode, but now a rat-infested building whose air was filled with the stench of urine and human excrement. As I climbed the steps, I reholstered my radio and unholstered my service revolver, not knowing what I would encounter on one of the floors. By the sound of the suspect's steps, I knew he was still climbing north and did not dart into one of the abandoned apartments. So I kept climbing two and three steps at a time hoping to gain on him. When we reached the fifth floor and were still climbing, I realized this guy was running on adrenaline only. As I tried to focus on the suspect, I also kept wondering if my partner was okay. Was he rolling around the sidewalk with the other guy? Nevertheless I had to remain focused on the one I was after. When I hit the landing between the fifth and sixth floor of the building, I heard the roof door slam shut. He went on the roof. It would be dark and unlit. I kept climbing. I wasn't going to give up now—or was I?

In all my years as a cop I never backed down from a situation, no matter how dangerous. This isn't a bravado statement, it's a statement of fact. The police could not back down. We were the thin blue line between civilization and chaos. When I took my oath of office I knew I would not have the privilege of running the other way in times of danger.

For some reason I stopped dead on the inside of the roof door and threw my back up against the wall. Why wasn't I going through the door? I knew he went out there. He's only a desperate junkie—and certainly not someone I couldn't take down. It was as if someone had his hand on my chest holding me back. I do not remember if I felt a physical presence stopping me or if it was something else that paralyzed me from gong one inch further. By now I was covered with perspiration. My heart was beating so hard I could actually see the center portion of my chest popping up and down and hear my heartbeat in my inner ears. I slid down the wall in a crouched position and called for a backup. They were there in a matter of minutes. There are no soldiers or police officers like those serving in the NYPD.

When two officers worked their way up to me, I told them what happened and for some reason I wasn't comfortable with going through the roof door. We unscrewed the light bulb on the landing for concealment as one of the backup officers swung open the door and held it open. As I shined my flashlight onto the roof landing I quickly noticed flattened discarded cardboard laid out just past the exit threshold of the doorway. I asked the second officer to keep his light trained on the cardboard as I pulled my nightstick from its holder. Stretching my nightstick through the doorway, I poked at the cardboard and watched pieces of it fall into a black abyss. The cardboard covered a hole in the roof approximately eight feet by five feet. The drop went down two stories into a pile of plaster, metal, and glass. It was a clever booby trap that the neighborhood felons knew about. Had I run through that door in hot pursuit of the bag snatcher, I would have fallen two stories either to my death or serious physical injury.

What was it that stopped me from going through that door? I had gone through more roof doors than I would like to remember and had never paused, never stopped. Why that time? Intuition? I don't think so, because that intuition never kicked in before during similar circumstances. Someone held me back from going through that door and onto the roof that evening. I am convinced to this very day, beyond a shadow of a doubt, that it was the hand of God, and perhaps a guardian angel, that prevented me from falling to my death. Nearly every time an angel appears in the Bible, the first words the angel says are, "Don't be afraid!" In some unspoken way those words were conveyed to me, "Don't be afraid; I've got your back."

Spiritual Warfare

I was working as the evening desk lieutenant in the 10th Precinct on the west side of Manhattan when a call came over the radio that two college students, a young couple, were stabbed in the back by a female who fled into her ground floor apartment after the assault. These two innocent kids were minding their own business walking north on 8th Avenue toward the Long Island Railroad terminal located beneath Madison Square Garden when a 400-pound, crazed woman charged them from behind shouting unintelligible words before she stabbed them both in the back with a kitchen knife. Thank God the two victims survived. After a brief standoff where the assailant barricaded herself in her apartment, members of the elite Emergency Services Unit broke down the door and apprehended this incredibly huge, strong, and crazed suspect. It required three pairs of handcuffs linked together to rear cuff this woman due to her size.

When she entered the station house her eyes were partially rolled up in the back of her head. She had white foam exuding from her mouth as she continued to babble an unintelligible grouping of phrases. I instructed the arresting officers to bring her up to the booking room and secure her in the holding pen. After 20 minutes one of the arresting officers came down to the front desk to inform me that she was not cooperating and was downright scary to handle. From the time she entered the precinct I sensed in my spirit that this woman was driven by something evil. So I had a sergeant relieve me on the desk and traveled up the stairs to where she was being held.

Entering the room I could smell a foul odor coming off of this woman. She was now shouting and bouncing off of the caged walls of the holding pen. The minute she spotted me she stared me down and gave me a steel cold look that made the hairs on the back of my neck stand up. All of my 175 pounds looked her right in the eyes, with both arresting officers watching. And then I said, "Sit down in the name of

Jesus." That was all I said. She backed up to the rear wall and sat down and we did not have a problem with her for the rest of the night until she was taken to a hospital for observation.

I know that is not standard police procedure. But there are some things in the spiritual realm that cannot be easily replicated as a procedure. Just as you would carefully suit up with the right equipment for patrol—it is equally, if not more, important to put on what the Bible calls the full armor of God, so that you can take your stand. What is the full armor of God, anyway?

"Put on the full armor of God so that you can take your stand against the devil's schemes. For our struggle is not against flesh and blood, but against the rulers, against the authorities, against the powers of this dark world and against the spiritual forces of evil in the heavenly realms. Therefore put on the full armor of God, so that when the day of evil comes, you may be able to stand your ground, and after you have done everything, to stand. Stand firm then, with the belt of truth buckled around your waist, with the breastplate of righteousness in place, and with your feet fitted with the readiness that comes from the gospel of peace. In addition to all this, take up the shield of faith, with which you can extinguish all the flaming arrows of the evil one. Take the helmet of salvation and the sword of the Spirit, which is the word of God. And pray in the Spirit on all occasions with all kinds of prayers and requests. With this in mind, be alert and always keep on praying for all the saints" (Ephesians 6:11-18).

Ironically, St. Paul was most likely chained to a Roman centurion when he wrote his description of the full armor of God. A centurion was like a first century police officer. And as Paul gazed at the soldier's armor he was inspired by the Holy Spirit to see in it the analogy of God's spiritual provision for our battle with Satan.[1] That is why Paul reminds us that "our struggle is not against flesh and blood, but against the rulers, against the authorities, against the powers of this dark world and against the spiritual forces of evil in the heavenly realms" (Ephesians 6:12-13).

So, when I think of what makes a good cop, I've come to believe that it has a spiritual dimension as well as a professional dimension. I knew I wanted to be equipped with God's spiritual armor.

FOUR

The Lighter Side of Policing

I don't want to leave the impression that being a cop is always heavy and serious. It has its lighter side.

The Nightstick Debacle

While walking a late night foot post in the South Bronx, I did all the things I saw police officers do when I was a kid growing up in Brooklyn. I checked storefront doors to make sure they were secure. I tipped my hat to passing persons. I made my calls to the station house. And, I twirled my nightstick—an act that required lots of practice and many bruises to my shin. The rawhide thong that threaded through the coco bolo nightstick was held in such a way that an officer could twirl the stick in a circular motion in front of him or shoot the nightstick out in front and then behind while drawing it back into his hand. That night I knew just enough about twirling a nightstick to be dangerous.

Standing in front of a Savings Bank on Burnside Avenue, I was twirling my nightstick in a frenzied pace due to boredom. First I twirled it side-to-side in front of my body and then forward and behind me in a sidewinder form. When the stick was thrown backward, there was a loud crash. I had broken the bank window, setting off the security alarm. It's hilarious to think of now, but I decided to run from the scene of the crime like a kid who just hit a home run through Mrs. Murphy's kitchen window. A short time later I was assigned to take the incident report. Too embarrassed to tell the supervisor what I did, I quickly took the assignment and completed the report on some notorious felon who tried to break into the bank.

23

It May Not Be What You Think

One night my partner Dominic and I were on routine patrol in the midtown area of Manhattan. Both of us were seasoned officers with a pretty keen eye for bad guys—even when bad guys try to look like good guys in a crowd. While traveling westbound on a side street, out of the corner of my eye, I noticed two males looking back in a very suspicious manner while moving briskly in and out between parked vehicles. It appeared that once the two spotted our radio car they crouched down behind a parked car in a hiding position. I told Dominic to stop the car and we both jumped out and grabbed these two suspected felons. Stretched out on the hood of a car, the older of the two turned around. Lo and behold, it was Ryan O'Neil, the famous actor, and his younger brother. What were they running from? It appeared that moments earlier, a group of admiring female fans had tried to rip their clothes off. My partner said to me, "Why is this never a problem for me?"

After a great chat with this friendly Hollywood celebrity, we reentered our patrol car. Dominic started laughing. I said, "What? What's so funny?" Shaking his head from side to side, he replied, "Charlie, you really know how to pick out those bad guys."

Ivan Putski, Lieutenant, NYPD

I was working with the Tactical Unit assigned to a security post around the perimeter of Madison Square Garden. That night there was a big professional wrestling event scheduled that drew a kind of crowd that tended to be unruly. It was a cold night and my partner and I decided to take a break inside the Garden. We worked our way through Garden security, right to the place where the wrestlers were preparing to enter the arena. There, standing in front of me, was the notorious Ivan Putski, one of the biggest attractions in professional wrestling at the time. Knowing that my father was an avid wrestling fan, I wished I had a camera with me to take a picture with this mammoth guy who had no neck. So I did the next best thing and asked him for his autograph. With nothing else to write on, I handed him my official memo book, thinking he would sign it on the back page of the official entry pages. I had placed rubber bands around the leather cover of the memo book so whenever I opened it, it would turn to the next available page for official entries. Ivan signed my book on the next entry line. Mind you, this memo book is admissible in a court of law and was an official police record—and Ivan Putsky signed it.

Later, the sergeant came around to give us a "scratch," meaning he would inspect us on post a minimum of two times during a tour of duty. In order to make his presence known, the supervisor signed an entry line by writing the time, his rank and signature, and shield number. Looking at my memo book, Sergeant Moreno asked me, "Who came to give you a scratch, Chuck?" I replied, "Oh, some lieutenant from the precinct named Krupski, Pupski, something like that." I gave Sergeant Moreno a salute and he drove off. And that was the night Ivan Putski was promoted to lieutenant in the New York City Police Department.

FIVE

The Root of Temptation

"But remember this—the wrong desires that come into your life aren't anything new and different. Many others have faced exactly the same problems before you. And no temptation is irresistible. You can trust God to keep the temptation from becoming so strong that you can't stand up against it, for he has promised this and will do what he says. He will show you how to escape temptation's power so that you can bear up patiently against it."
—St. Paul (1 Corinthians 10:13, TLB)

The officer who steps over the line and dishonors his oath of office by committing an unethical act says: "The money was right there—my partner and I were the only ones in the house besides the owner who was D.O.A.—he wouldn't notice the money missing and he certainly couldn't take it with him. I just couldn't resist."

The officer meets a beautiful woman on patrol. He's in his forties—the young lady is twenty-something. She's attracted to the uniform and flickers her flirtatious eyes. The officer is flattered that he can still draw the attention of a woman half his age. He loves his wife who is back home in the suburbs despite the fact that she has put on a few pounds and normally doesn't look all dolled up like the cutie making such advances. In his head he clearly hears "Don't do it"—but he says he couldn't resist the temptation and takes the first step toward an affair that will cost him his marriage and his family.

The officer has really been struggling at home with her husband. All he seems to do is sit on the couch, drink beer, and watch sports. It seems as if the life of their marriage is all but gone. By the time she gets to bed, her husband is already snoring. Her partner, whom she spends more time with than her husband, enjoys going to the gym, taking hikes in the mountains, and listening to Brazilian jazz. At first there was nothing there. They are both married and, hey, it's just a job. After several weeks she can see the conversation changing and she knows that she is slipping into feelings for the guy sitting next to her. She takes a glancing look at her partner and then draws an image of her husband on the couch.

When I examine myself, I find that I too am vulnerable to temptation—we all are. Who doesn't struggle with wanting to take a shortcut as a solution to quelling a human desire? It is hard to resist, isn't it? I cannot tell you how many times I have heard the words, "I just couldn't resist the temptation. I wanted to, but it was just too strong." The answer to that statement is, "True, you couldn't—but with help, you could have." The devil would have us believe that the fruit of evil is too irresistible to pass by. But God says differently. When we realize that God is not a tempter—and Satan is—then we at least know from where it comes and who our real opponent is.

Any good police officer worth his or her salt knows to remain alert at all times. You wouldn't let someone walk up behind you, or ever find yourself in a poor tactical position during a vehicle stop, would you? You even make sure you sit with your back to the wall when you go to a restaurant with your family, don't you? There is always a potential danger present in police work, even in the most routine assignment.

When a cadet enters the Police Academy, he or she learns some of the most sophisticated techniques of identifying and capturing criminals. Unfortunately, the one thing that cadets fail to learn is to identify the real suspect regarding crime, confusion, violence, and evil working in the communities they patrol. The law enforcement community does not hesitate to warn against terrorists, homicide suspects, and sexual predators. There are all kinds of composite drawings, mug shots, and modus operandi shared in the law enforcement community in order to capture persons responsible for violating the law that governs civility in our neighborhoods. And yet, the kingpin goes unmentioned and undetected. I think you know who I am referring to.

St. Paul says, "Run from anything that gives you the evil thoughts that young men often have, but stay close to anything that makes you want to do right" (2 Timothy 2:22, TLB). St. James says, "Submit yourselves, then, to God. Resist the devil, and he will flee from you.

Come near to God and he will come near to you" (James 4:7). This is a tailor-made tactical plan that no police academy instructor could have ever come up with. Pursue righteousness, faith, love, and peace. Submit to God and draw near to him. And once you have partnered up with God, you can then resist your most brutal opponent, Satan, and flee from the tempter's trap. That is the best E & E (Escape and Evasion) plan anyone can follow.

The Joseph Maneuver

The book of Genesis describes a young man named Joseph. He was handsome, young, well built, and very vulnerable. The wife of Potiphar, his master, noticed Joseph's attractiveness. Genesis 39:7 says, "And after a while his master's wife took notice of Joseph and said, 'Come to bed with me!'" It is no secret that physical attractiveness can provoke lust and desire. Joseph was not looking to have an affair. Actually, he was minding his own business. The Scripture proceeds to paint a picture of increased passion, lust, and seduction on the part of Potiphar's wife. This would have been a difficult place for any man to be. Joseph not only recognized that to have slept with her would have been a violation of his master's marriage, but it would have been a sin against God as well. He consistently refused her advances, giving no room for any idea on the part of the seducer that there was a chance to pull off this tryst. When he saw that she obviously would not take no for an answer, he fled from the house.

Police officers, even church-going police officers, may think they can handle integrity-challenging situations on their own. And I would say in most instances, they can. However, we all have weak moments just like the rest of the population. There may be a weakness with sex-related issues, materialism, self-promotion at any cost, or ego building. Whatever the weak area may be, it places the individual in a vulnerable position. The "Joseph Maneuver" is always the best tactic. Run from that which tempts you.

I vividly remember when I was a brand new narcotics investigator in the Organized Crime Control Bureau's 14th Narcotics Division in Brooklyn. My team hit a drug location with a search warrant in the tough Bedford Stuyvesant section. Our C.I. (confidential informant) provided us with a complete apartment floor plan—so each team member had an assigned room or section of the apartment to rush to once the forced entry was made. Our division was known as one of the best in taking down doors with a battering ram constructed out of a huge steel pipe with welded handles. City apartment doors are some of the most fortified entranceways in the world—especially when it is a known drug factory. There are deadbolts and an assortment of other locking devices running from top to bottom. Some of these locks were called "police locks." For most people this meant that the lock served as a police officer keeping thieves out of their premises. For drug dealers, a police lock is a device to keep the police out.

On our team was a huge, muscular, Mike Tyson-built African American detective whose name was Campbell. He was one of the most jovial persons I ever knew in the department. But when it came down to business, he loved two of the department's toys: the battering ram and the double-barrel shotgun. His eyes actually glowed when he held either instrument before a raid.

That afternoon our team leader and sergeant, affectionately known as "The Silver Fox" because of his silver hair, knocked on the door announcing we were the police and were in possession of a search warrant. There was a stirring inside like a bunch of rats exposed to a bright spotlight. We could easily hear the scurrying around, destruction of evidence, and some running to a rear window and fire escape. Campbell and another detective went right into action. Two blows with the battering ram and the door ripped open and our whole team piled in like paratroopers exiting the side door of a C-130. In the midst of loud shouting, "Police, don't move—get down—get down!" I was able to see in plain view on a coffee table at least a "key" (a kilo weighing 2.2 pounds) of heroin—the powder of death and destruction. There was a scale, envelopes, and mixing materials everywhere for the purpose of cutting, weighing, and packaging the drug for street sale and distribution. It turned out to be a major drug factory and the C.I.'s information was right for a change. We wound up with three occupants inside and one who was caught in the back alley by our back-up team as he jumped from the fire escape. Two handguns, one shotgun, and over three pounds of heroin were recovered that day.

My assignment was to run past the living room directly to a back bedroom, which I did. I pushed open the door, secured the room, and gazed over toward the dresser where there was a pile of packaged unmarked bills two feet wide and about nine inches high. Tens of thousands of dollars of unmarked U.S. currency in denominations of fives, tens, and twenties were just sitting there, waiting for a pick-up by a drug courier who would transfer the shipment to a dealer higher up in the drug organization.

Just for a fleeting moment—a flash of a thought—I wondered if it would be possible to fill my army field jacket pockets with thousands of dollars. For a split second, thoughts of a new car, a special vacation, and paying off the mortgage all entered my mind. There was no one else in the room with me. Everyone else was busy securing the prisoners and evidence or out the back window in pursuit of the one who fled the apartment. As my mind raced with very little effort—I yelled at the top of my lungs, "Sarge!" I knew that once someone else, especially a supervisor, witnessed the money, I would be all right.

The sergeant raced into the room with two other detectives thinking I was in trouble. They looked at me and all I did was point to the pile of money and said, "Look!" At that moment it felt as if the weight of the whole world lifted off of me. Who knows what might have happened had I lingered on that thought of temptation? The fruit was awfully attractive. Had I taken a single dollar bill it would have affected my life, my future decisions, and eventually my reputation and career.

King Solomon, one of the wisest men who ever lived, said, "Above all else, guard your heart, for it is the wellspring of life" (Proverbs 4:23). St. Paul wrote, "People who want to get rich fall into temptation and a trap and into many foolish and harmful desires that plunge men into ruin and destruction. For the love of money is a root of all kinds of evil. Some people, eager for money, have wandered from the faith and pierced themselves with many griefs" (1 Timothy 6:9-10).

SIX

Booze, Broads, and Bucks

Law Enforcement Code of Ethics[2]

As a law enforcement officer, my fundamental duty is to serve the community; to safeguard lives and property; to protect the innocent against deception, the weak against oppression or intimidation, and the peaceful against violence or disorder; and to respect the constitutional rights of all to liberty, equality, and justice.

I will keep my private life unsullied as an example to all and will behave in a manner that does not bring discredit to me or to my agency. I will maintain courageous calm in the face of danger, scorn, or ridicule; develop self-restraint; and be constantly mindful of the welfare of others. Honest in thought and deed both in my personal and official life, I will be exemplary in obeying the law and the regulations of my department. Whatever I see or hear of a confidential nature or that is confided to me in my official capacity will be kept ever secret unless revelation is necessary in the performance of my duty.

I will never act officiously or permit personal feelings, prejudices, political beliefs, aspirations, animosities, or friendships to influence my decisions. With no compromise for crime and with relentless prosecution of criminals, I will enforce the law courteously and appropriately without fear or favor, malice or ill will, never employing unnecessary force or violence and never accepting gratuities.

I recognize the badge of my office as a symbol of public faith, and I accept it as a public trust to be held so long as I am true to the ethics of police service. I will never engage in acts of corruption or bribery, nor will I condone such acts by other police officers. I will cooperate with all legally authorized agencies and their representatives in the pursuit of justice.

I know that I alone am responsible for my own standard of professional performance and will take every reasonable opportunity to enhance and improve my level of knowledge and competence.

I will constantly strive to achieve these objectives and ideals, dedicating myself before God to my chosen profession . . . law enforcement.

It's All about Integrity

In police work it is all about making choices. There are good choices and there are bad choices. And at the very heart of a right choice is a person's integrity. During my training at the police academy—in a class consisting of only male police officers—Lt. Crosby, one of the instructors, covered the area of integrity, though I do not believe he quite phrased it as such. With a twisted facial expression, he pointed to the sea of rookies clad in gray uniforms and asked, "Do you want to know the three things that will cost you your job?" Of course everyone nodded his head in the affirmative. He said, "It's real simple, boys: booze, broads, and bucks." Today, and rightfully so, this type of expression would not be acceptable—but back then everyone got the point. Most officers lose their jobs due to inappropriate behavior while drinking alcohol or getting involved in an improper relationship or for accepting a bribe. This is why integrity is a fundamental requirement for being a police officer.

Police officers must make a sincere commitment to a lifestyle of practicing good morals and maintaining their reputations—this is the image the public and our families must witness in the life of a police officer. Why? Police officers, like it or not, must live according to a higher standard than the general public. The paradox of law enforcement, unlike that of a firefighter, is that the general public does not always see a police officer as a helper. Firefighters are everybody's friend. This is not so when it comes to police officers. Firefighters, when not fighting fires, remain in the firehouse maintaining their equipment. Police officers, however, when not on a meal, are in the public view their entire shift. Remaining in public view no doubt acts as a deterrent to criminal activity and serves as a presence of security for the community, but it also leaves the officer on public display and under the careful observation and scrutiny of the public eye. There is no time for an officer to lay aside his or her professional presence.

I remember eating with my partner in an area diner when a woman across from us said to her friend, "Look, they're eating." To which my partner quickly replied, "Yeah, and we go to the bathroom, too!" My partner's response was uncalled for and he should have maintained his self-control—police officers need to get used to the fact that they are always under the watchful eye of the public.

Tony's Bad Choice

A precinct commander who once worked for me when I was a plainclothes supervisor called me at the church I was serving on Long Island. It was good to hear from him and to hear how well he was doing with his police career. This time he called to ask for some assistance with one of the police officers assigned to his command. Apparently this 29-year-old officer was married for eight years with two young daughters. His family lived in a modest house in a beautiful town on Long Island and everything seemed to be going well in this officer's career, family, and life. He even attended church regularly with his family.

It appeared that while on patrol in Queens he met a young lady who flirted with him. She was beautiful with a very shapely body and he agreed to meet her for a date. That date led to more involvement, so he decided to move in with her and her three small children. She supported herself as a stripper in a club in midtown Manhattan.

So what happened that an officer decided to leave his suburban house, his beautiful and faithful wife of eight years, and two daughters who worshiped the ground he walked on, and trade them in for an already-made family consisting of a stripper and three children fathered by two different men? How do you make sense of a decision like that—even if the woman was a debutante and heir to a fortune living in a penthouse on 5th Avenue?

The precinct commander asked if I would be willing to meet with the officer and, of course, I said yes. The appointment was set up for a Thursday morning in my office located at the church. When my secretary buzzed me over the intercom to advise me that my appointment had arrived, I said a quick prayer for wisdom and for this officer to be open to counsel.

In walked a good-looking young man with a pleasant smile. He looked like the most unsettled person in the world. I could tell he was very uncomfortable, but the first thing out of his mouth was that he would have never come to my office if I was just a minister. But because I was once on the job, he felt he could trust me.

Tony was an Italian-American who grew up in Bensonhurst, Brooklyn. His father was a retired cop who divorced his mother when he was 14 years old. Although his relationship with his father was friendly, they rarely spent quality time together. Tony's wife, Maureen, was Irish-American and grew up in the Bronx. Her father was an

35

active New York City firefighter. Both Maureen's parents were dead set against her marrying Tony in the first place. The Bronx Irish and Italians never got along and the thought of their daughter marrying an Italian cop's kid did not set well with them. The fact that Tony's parents were divorced and Maureen's parents were strict Roman Catholics didn't help.

After their wedding, Tony and Maureen secured an apartment in Brooklyn. Not too long after this, Tony tested for the position of police officer with the New York City Police Department. He scored high on the entrance exam and was hired a short time later. He attended the police academy and Maureen worked as an E.R. nurse at Brooklyn Methodist Hospital. With no children and a decent combined income, they were able to save up enough money for a down payment on a house in Medford, Long Island. It was a dream come true to own a home in the suburbs.

After Tony's graduation from the police academy, he was assigned to a Brooklyn precinct and Maureen transferred her nursing position to Mather Hospital in Port Jefferson. In two and a half years, Tony applied for a transfer to a Queens command, which would make his commute to and from work shorter, and he got it. Not only did it cut down on his travel time, it also placed him in a more relaxed environment than the high crime area he previously worked in. It seemed like the perfect scenario for Tony and Maureen.

During this time, a neighbor invited Tony and Maureen to attend her church. It was different from what they were used to with contemporary music and a young and dynamic preacher. The couple fell in love with the church and the people. There were a lot of young couples and children and the environment was more family-oriented. Even though both Tony's and Maureen's families were Roman Catholic and both were christened, received first communion, and confirmed—neither one had practiced their faith since confirmation training. Their neighbor's church filled the missing pieces in their lives. They now had great Christian friends and more importantly, both became very serious about their faith. They even began studying the Bible as a couple. Tony attended men's meetings when he could and Maureen was active with the women's ministry.

Almost four years after they were married, their first child was born—a beautiful baby girl they named Elizabeth. Two years after that, their second daughter was born whom they named Courtney. It was a Norman Rockwell-scene out of the *Saturday Evening Post*—a beautiful home, a beautiful couple, two beautiful children, a good job, and a great church.

Now, two years later, Tony was living in a three-bedroom apartment in Jackson Heights, Queens with a stripper and three of her children. What could have possibly gone wrong? How could a loyal husband, father, and Christian make such a radical change?

As I looked across at Tony, who had his head bowed most of the time, I asked him how it all happened. How did he get from Medford, Long Island to Jackson Heights, Queens? He told me that he first met his live-in girlfriend on a domestic dispute between her and a male companion who was living there. The male was domineering, macho, and abusive. So when Tony arrived on the scene, took charge, and put the guy in his place—the boyfriend said he was taking his belongings and leaving with a promise never to return. He kept that promise. To this woman, Tony was a knight in shining armor. He was sympathetic, caring, and gentle with her—though he was very professional and not flirtatious at all. He advised her that if the man ever returned to call the station and a police officer would be dispatched to assist her.

Apparently she had read his nametag and the next day during his shift went to the station house and asked the desk lieutenant to see him about her case. The lieutenant called Tony off of patrol and advised him that there was a woman waiting to see him in the back room. To Tony's surprise, it was Gloria.

She explained to him how she could not sleep all night thinking about how helpful Tony was and how much she appreciated him. He replied with a smile that he was only doing his job. She told him that she was the best cook in all of Queens and would like to repay him with a scrumptious Latino dinner. It was at that point Tony lost control of his common sense and spiritual discernment and accepted the invitation to dinner for the following week.

To keep the date hidden from his wife, Tony put in for the night off using a vacation day, hid some nice clothes in the trunk of his car, and changed at the precinct before going over to Gloria's apartment.

When Tony arrived, he told me that Gloria answered the door looking like a model from a men's magazine. Her hair was beautifully made up, dress fitted and sexy, and lips were painted and sensual. He found her absolutely irresistible. He noticed that her children were not around. She told him they were staying at her mother's house for the weekend and that they would be undisturbed to enjoy their dinner together.

Although Tony did not normally drink, Gloria had a good Merlot wine on the table that he drank in gulps trying to build up the courage for whatever was going to happen that night. He was also hoping to deaden his conscience.

After their dinner together, they both cleaned up the dishes and Gloria lowered the lights and put on some romantic music as they took their places on the couch—and the rest is history. Tony soon found himself calling Gloria nearly every hour of the day. He would visit her during his meal breaks and vacation days. When he was home, he discovered his mind was totally occupied with thoughts of Gloria and not Maureen.

Things went from bad to worse. He found fault in the most minor things Maureen did. He told his wife that he no longer wanted to attend church. He soured on his faith and even accused his Christian friends of being weaklings who used religion as a crutch to escape reality. His sexual life with Maureen decreased and became more perfunctory as he became increasingly distant from her. It was important for him to tell me that he never stopped showing affection toward his two daughters.

Maureen was desperate and called Tony's father, but he told his daughter-in-law that his son's behavior went with the territory of living with a cop. Maureen refused to call her parents, knowing they were never really fond of Tony in the first place. She was afraid to tell her pastor or her friends and made all kinds of excuses for why Tony was never around. She was stuck at home with two children, no longer working, and wondering what she could have done so wrong to have upset her husband this way. She could not see that his behavior had nothing to do with her.

One day while the children were asleep, Tony broke the news to Maureen that the job and the commute to the city was causing too much stress and pressure and he wanted to try a separation and live in the city to "find himself." Maureen was devastated, but she thought if he had a little time alone he would come to his senses and realize that he needed his family—so she agreed to let him go. The next day he loaded up his car and drove down the driveway headed toward Queens, not to live alone, but to move in with Gloria and her three children.

Now Tony was sitting in my office not knowing what to do. Gloria was putting a lot of pressure on him to file for divorce, while Maureen and the girls were waiting for him to return home. He was living a big lie and he knew it. His state of confusion was affecting his job performance and his health.

SEVEN

Maintaining Integrity

"Always do the right thing, kid," Sergeant Hank Edwards, Tactical Patrol Force, NYPD, would always say to me. During my years as an officer assigned to the T.P.F. (Tactical Police Force), I had the pleasure of working under the guidance and leadership of an old time sergeant who entered the department right after the Korean War. Sergeant Henry "Hank" Edwards was from the old school where you were taught to work hard, never disgrace your family or department, and always do the right thing. If I heard Hank say that phrase once, I heard him say it hundreds of times over the years. Not too many years ago I had the opportunity to call Hank who retired years ago with over 35 years on the job. Now his health is deteriorating due to acute diabetes. He's going blind and it's hard to imagine remembering what a craftsman he was in building beautiful pieces of furniture. Wouldn't you know, just as we were saying our goodbyes, old Hank said, "Chuck, I always liked you, my friend. Remember to do the right thing."

God takes great pleasure in those who exhibit a life of integrity and who do the right thing. In Psalm 15 the psalmist David defines who God takes pleasure in: "He whose walk is blameless and who does what is righteous, who speaks the truth from his heart and has no slander on his tongue, who does his neighbor no wrong and casts no slur on his fellowman, who despises a vile man but honors those who fear the Lord, who keeps his oath even when it hurts, who lends his money without usury and does not accept a bribe against the innocent. He who does these things will never be shaken."

A person of integrity and good character is one whose walk is blameless and who does what is righteous. Integrity and good character is at the very core of what it means to do the right thing. I

41

firmly believe there are lots of honest people who in and of themselves greatly fail in this area. Why? Because living a righteous life requires a dependency on one who is completely righteous.

Integrity encompasses a wide range of behaviors. It is not merely rejecting a bribe or resisting taking something that doesn't belong to you. It is being obedient to your superiors. It is honoring and respecting others and their property. It is telling the honest truth and not distorting or embellishing the facts. It is having the reputation of being dependable. It is being punctual and prepared. It is being loyal to those you have promised to be loyal to. It is being moral in all situations. It is practicing fairness in dealing with others. It is being humble and not thinking of yourself more highly than you ought. It is being decisive and making those decisions based on what is right, rather than what is popular or easy. It is maintaining self-control by keeping your thoughts, words, deeds, and attitude under a moral code. It is being courageous in the face of difficult or unpopular circumstances. I know it sounds like an insurmountable quest, but this list is endless as to what a life of integrity should look like in the life of a police officer. Short of my salvation, integrity is what I treasure and guard the most in my life. I believe that when people lose their integrity, they lose their witness.

I remember a new teller in our local bank giving me $50 too much in my change. She should have given me five ten dollar bills, but instead gave me five twenties. As I drove off through the drive-thru and stopped to get a cup of coffee and gas up my car, I noticed the mistake. With God's help, the decision was easy. I immediately drove back over to the bank, and discretely got the attention of the young teller and advised her of her mistake, returning to her my change and receipt just as she had given it to me moments earlier. Not only was it the right thing to do and what God would want, but it also brought great comfort and peace to another individual, which made my entire day. The clerk was both delighted and surprised. It could have been so easy to justify not going back. I could have said that going back would have made me late for my next appointment, or the bank could afford a measly $50 with all the money they have. No one would have known. Well, that may be true. Perhaps no one would have known—no earthly person, that is. But God would have known. And integrity has everything to do with when people are watching and when they are not.

The great nineteenth century preacher, Dwight L. Moody, once said, "Character is what you are in the dark."[3] A daily devotional reading captures the essence of maintaining our integrity at all times. "Nothing is quite as comforting—and at the same time quite disconcerting—as the truth that God knows everything. He knows your thoughts; he knows your actions; he knows your words. He knows when you get up and when you go to bed. He understands your motives and intentions even when no one else on earth does. But at the same time he knows your secret sins that no one else ever sees: pride, lust, jealousy, coveting. And he holds you just as accountable for your secret sins as for those that others know about. Similarly, God's presence can be both a comfort and a concern. There is no mountain you can climb, or depth you can descend, where he is not there. His presence shines through the darkness and transcends distance. But at the same time, that puts the lie to any notion of 'secret sins' you can commit without his being there. His presence with you is persistent."[4]

The moment I lifted my change from the bank off of the front seat of my car and counted it, it was clear to me that God was present. That is why the W.W.J.D. (What Would Jesus Do?) items have marketed so well. People know how weak they really are in the face of tough decisions. And having a reminder, even a bracelet, helps us to remember that we are accountable to a higher standard.

The Bible makes sure to remind us to do the right thing:

- "Do what is right and good in the Lord's sight, so that it may go well with you" (Deuteronomy 6:18).
- "Blessed are they who maintain justice, who constantly do what is right" (Psalm 106:3).
- "Be careful to do what is right in the eyes of everybody" (Romans 12:17b).
- "For we are taking pains to do what is right, not only in the eyes of the Lord but also in the eyes of men" (2 Corinthians 8:21).
- "And as for you, brothers, never tire of doing what is right" (2 Thessalonians 3:13).

The genius of Mark Twain cannot be denied. His outlook on life, though frequently comical, was often packed with great insight and wisdom. He once said, "Always do what is right. This will surprise some people and astonish the rest."[5] There was a time in our culture when the right thing was assumed and quite frankly, expected. Today, doing what is right and what is moral is often unexpected and indeed astonishing. I believe the bank clerk was no doubt pleased, but her facial expressions and body language showed surprise and astonishment that someone would actually return to make things right.

St. Paul said it so well, "Therefore, I urge you, brothers, in view of God's mercy, to offer your bodies as living sacrifices, holy and pleasing to God—this is your spiritual act of worship. Do not conform any longer to the pattern of this world, but be transformed by the renewing of your mind. Then you will be able to test and approve what God's will is—his good, pleasing and perfect will" (Romans 12:1-2).

Cadets at the United States Military Academy at West Point follow an Honor Code that was established in the early 1800s and is still as much a part of the fabric of their institution as it was almost 200 years ago. The code simply, but profoundly, states: "A cadet will not lie, cheat, steal, or tolerate those who do."[6] Think about applying such a simplistic, yet powerful code of honor in your personal life and duty as a Christian police officer. There is a definite Code of Honor that is established all throughout the pages of the Bible that reinforces the vow that a first-year plebe pledges to abide by.

Broad Is the Road
That Leads to Destruction

Police officers, just by the very nature of their job, must always be in control of every situation while on the street. It is the police who keep the peace instead of a reign of chaos. If drivers didn't fear a State Trooper hiding behind some knoll on the highway, they would most likely travel at speeds of 10, 20, 30 MPH, or even higher over the speed limit. If our police departments lost control of order in our communities, there would be extreme disorder and not a single citizen would be safe in his or her home or to venture outside and walk the streets.

It is important for police officers to maintain control of their environment—but that has to do with tactics and not necessarily that of living a God-led life. Left up to our own flesh instincts that are inherent in every human being, we would be led down paths in life with the potential and high probability of great harm and eventual destruction.

Jesus said, "Enter through the narrow gate. For wide is the gate and broad is the road that leads to destruction, and many enter through it. But small is the gate and narrow the road that leads to life, and only a few find it" (Matthew 7:13). Life is made up of many decisions and the choices we make reveal our inner nature—what we are made of, our character.

The broad and narrow way Jesus spoke of places into contrast a life that lives for God and a life that lives for self. By nature human beings are generally selfish individuals. "What's in it for me?" and "What's the bottom line for me?" are questions commonly heard amongst discussions in our culture. There is a natural propensity toward making selfish decisions. Many Americans are in search of the abundant life that consists of more money and the accumulation of more things. This is what often drives an individual's decision—self-gratification, self-pleasure, self-absorption. But Jesus says in John 10:10, "I am come that you might have life, and have it more abundantly." However, the abundant life Jesus offers does not come without discipline and self-restraint. The late Bishop Fulton Sheen once said, "The difference between a river and a swamp is that the river has borders and the swamp has none." We must be selective in our behavior patterns. The broad road is filled with people who do whatever they feel like doing. The narrow road is traveled by individuals who call upon God to lead them to make decisions that are not necessarily self-pleasing, but God-pleasing.

No matter how tactically astute and brave a police officer may be, each and every one of us is vulnerable to make bad choices concerning ethics and morality. Given the right circumstances, any one of us is capable of committing almost any violation imaginable. St. Paul, perhaps the greatest champion for faith in the history of the church, writes: "Christ Jesus came into the world to save sinners—of whom I am the worst" (1 Timothy 1:15). If Paul knew he was a sinner and struggled with his flesh every day—what makes us think we can just breeze through life without the awareness of such a sinful nature in ourselves?

In the NYPD, there is a code that holds the highest priority for response over any other code—a signal 10-13. This means that there is an officer in trouble. When it is heard over the portable radio of a foot cop—that officer will flag down a taxi, commandeer a private vehicle, or run at top speed to respond to his or her comrade in need. Officers in sector cars will drop everything, dump coffee cups, and pardon a speeder they were just about to ticket—to jump in their vehicle and race to a brother or sister officer's cry for help. There is nothing so beautiful sounding when you are rolling on the ground with someone than hearing the once annoying, but now melodic, sound of a police siren getting louder and closer as it moves in your direction. You instantly know to hold on a little longer because help is coming and soon you will be out of harm's way.

The same is true when we are entering harm's way due to temptation. An officer needs to call a signal 10-13—that is, 1 Corinthians 10:13. This passage of Scripture will lead a person out of trouble every time. The Apostle Paul wrote, "But remember this—the wrong desires that come into your life aren't anything new and different. Many others have faced exactly the same problems before you. And no temptation is irresistible. You can trust God to keep the temptation from becoming so strong that you can't stand up agianst it, for he has promised this and will do what he says. He will show you how to escape temptation's power so that you can bear up patiently against it" (Corintians 10:13, TLB).

EIGHT

A Cop's Family Life

The police officer has a hard job, but the officer's family often has a harder one.

Great Families Don't Just Happen

The spouse of a police officer is an extraordinary being. There is an enormous amount of sacrifice and unselfishness required on the part of one who is married to a cop. The work is demanding and often stressful. The shift work goes counter-culture and disrupts a normal family routine. This is why a police officer and the family of a police officer must be an informed family to increase the odds of not only succeeding in a difficult life, but doing so with peace and joy.

In *The Book of Virtues*, Bill Bennett includes "work" as one of the top ten virtues in life. *Webster's Dictionary* defines work, in part, as "sustained physical or mental effort to overcome obstacles and achieve an objective or result." What does the average cop try to achieve through his or her work? What is it that satisfies through accomplishment? What drives a person to become a police officer and remain in the profession until retirement? Great pay? Probably not. Good benefits? Perhaps. Pride in being part of a team? Most likely. Adventure? Yes. A chance to make a difference in your community? I would hope so. The opportunity for advancement? Better than most places. A chance to regularly change assignments and remain with the same employer? Absolutely.

There are numerous reasons why one would decide to become a police officer. Unlike the 1950s and 1960s when recruits entered the police force for job security, today's recruit most likely enters police work simply because he or she is attracted to the vocation. As I shared earlier, I wanted to be a police officer ever since I can remember. I

47

was always intrigued with TV programs like *Dragnet*, *Highway Patrol*, *Adam-12*, *The F.B.I.*, *Naked City*, and even *Gun Smoke* with Marshal Dillon. But what I really had to learn was that being a police officer was only a job—a place of employment and not my whole life. That if I allowed it to happen, my police role could have consumed my entire life and occupied my thoughts both on and off duty—and it did for a season. The need for balance, especially in the life of a police officer, is absolutely essential if you are going to keep a family together.

Plain and simple, the life of an officer's family is often a difficult one. Police work makes extraordinary demands on the family. Cops are for the most part underpaid, overworked, and intentionally dispatched to controversial and dangerous places no one else wants to go. Crazy hours, subpoenas to court during off-duty time, overtime details, and unexpected shift hold-overs all add to the difficulty of life within the police family.

"Police officers want an ordered society where it is safe for their wives and children; they want to help those who need assistance and are too weak to protect or help themselves; they want the satisfaction of serving mankind but without any possible stigma of being a sissy," writes Dorothy Fagerstrom, one-time research editor for *Law and Order Magazine*. "They expect their wives and families to understand that this is something they must do and to approve. They present a rough, tough exterior to the world; yet behind that exterior, they have hearts as big as all outdoors and they are sentimental softies."[7]

Oftentimes, however, many of the difficulties experienced are self-imposed. For a good part of my police career, my wife put up with my involvement in an adulterous relationship. Yes, I cheated on my wife. My mistress, however, was the job. Why is this so prevalent in the lives of so many police officers?

We live in a culture where success takes first place. Life in the workplace has become increasingly more difficult with greater deadlines, statistical comparisons, heightened productivity expectations, and a plethora of other pressures. Success, especially in America, is defined and measured by the house we live in, the kind of car we drive, and the clothes we wear. As a result, the family that was once the core of a person's life and identity has been sadly replaced by a job—because a job defines self-worth.

The image of a father returning home at the end of a work day with a lunch pail in his hand, greeted at the door by his wife, children, and the family dog as a prelude to all of them sitting down for a family dinner and time of sharing, laughter, and instruction is all but gone. Although my fond memories of growing up are probably greater than the actual experience, I still vividly remember awakening each morning to a prepared breakfast before heading off for school. Granted, my father was already up and on his way to work. He was a machine mechanic who repaired huge factory machinery that produced cardboard boxes for major department stores. We lived in a very poor section of Williamsburgh, Brooklyn, in a four-story tenement building with a monthly rent of $28. I always said that if you fired one shot at one end of the apartment you would hit the whole family. Next to the radiator in the living room was a plumber's wrench that wasn't used for plumbing, but rather to tap the radiator so the landlord would receive this ancient form of signaling two stories below and hopefully turn up the heat. And once one of the tenants started banging on the pipes, every other apartment dweller in the building would join in the cacophony of blended sounds of metal striking metal.

We didn't have a whole lot in comparison to today's standard of living. Yet my dad traveled by public transportation (we never owned a family car) from Brooklyn to Elizabeth, New Jersey, every single day to scratch out a living for his family. When he was spotted by one of us from our fourth floor perch slowly lumbering down the street toward our building, a yell went out through the apartment as if it were a sailor shouting from a ship's crow's nest that land was spotted: *"Dad's home!"* The family dog, Peggy, with her tail wagging like a metronome, ran down the four flights of steps to greet my dad halfway. You could hear him laughing as she licked his face like a windshield wiper set on high speed. Dad was home!

My dad worked 50 hours a week, spent six hours commuting, and brought home $60 a paycheck—but it was enough to keep us all together as a family unit. I don't know how my mother timed it, but as soon as he arrived home, a delicious meal would miraculously appear on the table to be consumed by an appreciative family.

The Ferrara family was not perfect by any stretch of the imagination. In fact, there was a lot to be desired. Yet, it was great to come home from school each day knowing Mom was there to greet us and to know that Dad would be home in three hours to start the evening ritual and festivities. As I did my homework it was very comforting to hear the pots and pans banging in the kitchen as Mom prepared our dinner. The aroma of a special sauce or a baked turkey added to the anticipation of gathering for the evening meal. Can this Norman Rockwell-type scene ever be recaptured by the modern day family? Perhaps not exactly; but I would suggest that with a purposeful desire to create quality family time, a similar environment is possible. This is especially important for the police family. In order to have a family, it all begins with a husband and a wife.

When Two Become One

"Men marry women hoping they will not change. Women marry men hoping they will change."[8]

Lenny was a young, bright, and genuinely sincere sergeant. He had been proudly wearing his chevrons for about one year. He was an intense kind of guy who took his job very seriously. I wish I could report the same about his marriage.

Lenny loved his toys. Some guys love guns, others drool over a car—Lenny had a love for boats. He enjoyed fishing and sailing along the waterways. His time on the water provided him with a sense of freedom and a getaway from the pressures of the job. The only problem, that freedom he enjoyed had a negative impact on his young wife of only two years. Because Lenny was not provided a positive male role model growing up—a figure that provided the proper care, respect and attention to his spouse—almost everything Lenny did surrounded his interests. So he discovered what he thought was happiness in the things he purchased and accumulated.

Do you think Lenny is alone in this area? I can tell you from life's experiences and an endless number of hours counseling troubled couples, Lenny is a typical baby boomer, baby buster, and most likely Generation X husband. If you asked Lenny the question, "Lenny, do you love Carol?" he would snap back without hesitation, "Of course I do, why?" And you know what? He genuinely does. However, he just was never properly equipped, taught, or given direction on tangible ways to let his wife know that he loved her. When your spouse is driving a car that breaks down every hundred miles and you purchase a new boat to play on—the message you communicate, even though you may not feel that way, is, "I don't care if you safely arrive to your destination or not, just as long as I have my big toy to play with."

Lenny's wife, Carol, came in to see me one afternoon; she was obviously at her wit's end. She loved Lenny, but after two years of marriage she was beginning to wonder if things would get worse before they ever got better. Lenny was into buying and maintaining big toys—yet, if she purchased a twelve dollar blouse, Lenny would give her the third degree and go off on a 20-minute dissertation on how financially strapped they were.

During the holidays or on special occasions, Lenny knew what kind of gift would make Carol happy—yet he couldn't bring himself to drive to the mall and buy it. Even though Lenny knew the gift would not cost much and certainly could never match the expenditures he made to support his hobbies, Carol's happiness was rarely his priority. Time after time, Carol lifted her hopes only to be let down. Sometimes Lenny would even forget to buy a card or a dozen roses for her birthday or their anniversary. Dinner dates were rare and quality time was non-existent.

As she sat across from me, she wondered if she married the right guy. She wondered what had happened to the guy who once showered her with love and affection before they married.

Earlier I shared how I committed adultery on my wife—not with another woman, but with my job as my mistress. In his book *Boundaries in Marriage*, Dr. Henry Cloud defines adultery as much more than just sharing your body sexually with someone other than your spouse. One can commit "emotional adultery," meaning that you take aspects of yourself and intentionally keep them away from your marriage.[9] Lenny was doing exactly that, and he is not alone. Many partners in marriage today are avoiding their spouses by being drawn away to other people, things, and activities. It doesn't necessarily have to be a boat that sails on a waterway far away from the house. There are spouses who become emotionally detached without ever leaving the house, simply by surfing the internet—one of today's greatest detractors in marriages. For many it turns into an addiction, with exorbitant time spent in chat rooms feeding fantasy relationships.

The autonomy and convenience of sitting in front of a computer monitor leads many people to access pornography. This addiction often leads to a significant battle in the lives of many married couples. I strongly recommend that if you are struggling with an addiction to pornography, pick up Stephen Arterburn's book, *Every man's battle: A Guide to Winning the War on Sexual Temptation One Victory at a Time.*

When left unchecked, such forces can contribute to the eventual breakdown of a marital relationship. As already mentioned, some of these competing detractors can be a job, hobbies, the internet, career development, or an extramarital affair. It can also be too much time spent on the telephone, in front of the television, with friends, the children, or even serving at the local church. Remember, I am not suggesting, other than the extramarital affair and pornography, that any of these are in and of themselves, bad. On the other hand, when our spouse takes second or third place in the scheme of things, and we deprive them of the necessary care, time, and attention—our life becomes out of balance and a strong possibility of marital trouble begins to develop.

Stephen Covey once wrote, "The way you spend your time is a result of the way you see your time and the way you really see your priorities."[10]

Remember that the things that are most important to us will impact the choices we make in using our time and resources. If God and family are most important to us—we will pour ourselves in these areas. This doesn't mean that we will have no time for ourselves or for our job. It just means that God should impact every area of our lives and everything we do, whether we are at work or play, but especially in our family life.

Egocentricities in Marriage

The average person wants to live a life of happiness and peace. In fact, to not desire this would be abnormal. There is nothing wrong with this desire, unless it takes the form of self-centeredness. Living a self-centered life, especially in marriage, has a reverse effect, diminishes the happiness and peace of our spouse, and creates a formula for disaster in that relationship.

A healthy marriage involves sacrifices and a give-and-take relationship. There are times when we should refrain from doing what we please in order to accommodate our spouse's wishes. Myong Cha, my wife, likes to shop for clothes. Actually, she doesn't just like it—she revels in it. On the other hand, I like sports memorabilia shops, bookstores, and antique galleries. There are times when I bite my lower lip and enter the women's department with my wife and walk alongside of her as she touches every garment, places dresses up to her body, and tries on dozens of outfits. She comes out of the dressing room dozens of times asking me the same question: "What do you think, honey?"

And each time I reply with the same answer, "It looks great—it's really you." She does look great in almost anything—and I can still say that after being married to her for 37 years. We usually leave the store without a purchase, but my wife is happy by just experiencing the mall. But then she will accompany me as I play with a Derek Jeter bobble head doll or try on a Yankees warm-up jacket. Then it becomes my turn, "Honey, what do you think?" And she'll reply, "It's all you, honey. Quick, somebody call Joe Torre—you're ready to go into the game!" It is all about sacrifice. It is about give and take.

Jesus said, "...In the beginning the Creator 'made them male and female,' and said, 'For this reason a man will leave his father and mother and be united to his wife, and the two will become one flesh.' So they are no longer two, but one. Therefore what God has joined together, let man not separate" (Matthew 19:4-6).

When two become one, it means that what happens to one of you will affect the other. When my wife is happy, I am at my happiest. When she is sad, I am deeply saddened. When she suffers, I suffer greatly. I love her so much because she is part of who I am. We may be two individual people, but spiritually and emotionally, we are one and therefore what happens to one affects the other.

What Jesus was saying, by referring to a passage taken from the book of Genesis, is that when a couple gets married, they leave the home of their parents and form a whole new family. A beautiful transition occurs where, as only God would have it, two persons, from two different backgrounds, having grown-up under two separate roofs, and are united as one under divine blessing.

A good marriage involves a sacrificial relationship. It is not all about me—it's about us as a couple, a team, a unit. In the Bible, St. Paul instructs husbands to love their wives as Christ loved the church; and we know that Jesus sacrificed his very life for the church. This involves a willingness to lay it all down and sacrifice our entire life for our life-partner, our spouse. If I asked the average husband or wife if he or she was placed in a situation that required giving up their physical life to save the life of their spouse, would they? I believe in most cases the answer would be yes, without hesitation. That situation rarely happens, however. But successful and happy marriages do require dying to ourselves in order to be a living sacrifice for the one we love. Simply, we die in order to live—to live for our spouse. It requires humility and not always getting our way. It calls for us to

53

seek our spouse's happiness over our own—because when our spouse is happy, we should be happy. A sacrificial husband or wife not only finds opportunities to make his or her spouse happy, but also looks for ways to encourage them in ways that build up, and not tear down. We should be our spouse's greatest cheerleader, rather than being his or her greatest critic.

When a starry-eyed couple comes to my office and announces they want to get married, yes, there is a sense of loving affection between the two of them. However, the greatest drive to the altar is a physical attraction toward one another. I'm happy to say that the ones who have a strong Christian faith base possess a greater love that reaches beyond themselves. God's love reigning within them is evident and a big part of the equation. They understand the importance of a covenantal relationship and what that relationship requires going into their marriage plans. But sadly, most couples do not. They enter the relationship on attraction and feelings—both are good, but neither will sustain a marriage.

NINE

Giving Your Marriage a Prayer

I can't think of any practice that is more effective in marriage than prayer. There is real power when a husband and wife pray together. The old adage is true: "Couples who pray together, stay together." Couples who frequently pray together are twice as likely as those who pray less often to describe their marriages as being highly romantic. And married couples who pray together are 90 percent more likely to report higher satisfaction with their sex lives than couples who don't pray together.[11] That result in and of itself is a good reason to pray together.

I recently attended a presentation where one of the speakers shared that even though the divorce rate is 50 percent outside the church and 49 percent inside the church—couples who regularly pray together have a divorce rate of less than one percent.[12] That is an incredible statistic and enormous indicator that prayer is the glue that keeps a marriage together. Make a commitment to pray together on a daily basis. Don't make it difficult or complicated. Find a quiet time and space where you can hold hands and pray for one another. Don't use the time to give sermons on what you want your spouse to hear and change. Speak directly to God and make your desires and thankfulness known to him.

When Jesus prayed, he taught us to use simple, uncomplicated statements and requests. Prayer doesn't require eloquent Elizabethan English to be effective. All it requires is that you approach God with a reverent attitude, asking him to meet your daily needs, to forgive your sins, and to keep you from situations where you may be tempted to sin. You can approach God like he is a loving parent, knowing that you have his full attention. Oftentimes we discover ourselves anxious in our marriages, about the relationship, the finances, and the kids.

God gives us the answer during these times: "Do not be anxious about anything, but in everything, by prayer and petition, with thanksgiving, present your requests to God. And the peace of God, which transcends all understanding, will guard your hearts and your minds in Christ Jesus" (Philippians 4:6-7). Isn't that what you are really pursuing in life?

What humanity seeks the most in life is peace. When we have peace, we have joy and strength and hope. Buying a new car or making some other purchase brings us temporary peace and joy—but it soon wears off. Prayer brings us peace that transcends all understanding because it comes from the Prince of Peace. This peace is very different from what the world offers. In fact, Jesus himself said, "Peace I leave with you; my peace I give you. I do not give to you as the world gives. Do not let your hearts be troubled and do not be afraid" (John 14:27).

Dr. Tim Kimmel, an author and daily Christian radio host, compiled a list of ways to love your spouse. You must know how to act out the love that you have for them:[13]

- Assume responsibility for your actions and be quick to say, "I'm sorry," and "Forgive me."
- Follow through on commitments.
- Frequently tell your spouse what you like about him or her (be specific).
- Go over the upcoming week, anticipating pressure points.
- Praise your spouse in public.
- Remember key holidays and occasions.
- Give your spouse time to be by themselves.
- Encourage your spouse to cultivate deep and supportive friendships.

Part of being intimate and respectful to your spouse is providing them with the courtesy of keeping them in the loop of your life. None of the points mentioned above by Dr. Kimmel are very difficult to place into practice and maintain. It requires a genuine willingness to be sacrificial. Try implementing these steps and see the spark that you will engender in your marriage.

I am still learning, after many years of marriage, how to be a good husband. It is an ongoing process, but over time the practice makes it increasingly more natural. Husbands, we need to give ourselves an attitude check on a regular basis. Are you building up your wife on a consistent basis? Are you respecting her uniqueness? Are you giv-ing her individual and loving attention? Are you lavishing her with thoughtful gifts? Are you participating in the life and the care of the things that go on inside the house?

Good marriages don't just happen—they require work and careful attention. I have discovered that it is the little things that count. Each and every morning I make the coffee and bring a cup to my wife just the way she likes it. She appreciates that more than if I bought her a brand new car. She will often brag to other women how I make her coffee each morning. It is my absolute delight to do this for my wife because it stems from the love I have for her. My wife likes to prepare our bed each night and fluffs up the pillows and turns down the sheets or puts on the heating blanket—and it is done just for me. She wants our bed to be welcoming and comfortable when I get ready to go to sleep. These little things have become rituals of love that both of us enjoy doing and receiving. Find little ways to do things for your spouse as signs of your love and affection for him or her.

Learn How to Disengage in order to Engage

Learn how to engage in some healthy hobbies to keep your mind on things and topics other than police work. Consider taking a class on photography or oil painting. Take a stab at model building or join a Civil War reenactment group if history whets your appetite. Speaking of appetite, consider taking up gourmet cooking or baking. Read up on and try your hand at hiking, kayaking, golf, tennis, rack-etball, hunting, cycling, jogging, or martial arts.

I know an officer who likes to go antique browsing with his wife on his days off. They may not buy something on every outing, but they get to travel along the beautiful upper Hudson River in New York State or through small towns in Pennsylvania and share a lunch date together. This keeps their marriage healthy and filled with the antici-pation of their next journey together. Another couple enjoys going to the shooting range together while another officer and her husband collect coins and stamps.

Be careful not to become so consumed by your work that you lose sight of the other parts of life which make up the whole person. An unhealthy obsession can easily develop to the point of hanging out with other cops talking about the job, even outside of work. Try to make friends with others who work in different professions than your own. One officer told me that he only hangs out with cops because there is no defending of the job or explaining what it's like to be a cop. He said cops understand each other from the onset of the relationship. They work the same shifts and deal with the same elements that a guy working for IBM just doesn't understand. That may be true, but common denominators in relationships are not just discovered in police work. A great place to make friends outside of the job is in the church.

There are several police officers and police dispatchers who attend the church I pastor, and they thoroughly enjoy the relationships they have made with others who simply share the common denominator of faith. One detective sergeant especially enjoys organizing short-term mission trips to Costa Rica. On his most recent trip he bonded with a Culligan Water Systems supervisor and a retired Nestle executive. Because of his active church participation, although he is a good and effective street detective supervisor, he is very comfortable mixing with people from all kinds of occupational backgrounds.

There are, no doubt, some pros to cops hanging out with other cops and their families. There are some setbacks as well. One officer recently told me that he doesn't like his wife chumming up with other police officers' wives because they manage to share information and misinformation that leads to increased fear, misunderstanding, and suspicion. As a chaplain I once sat at a police social where a wife who had a couple of drinks actually said to a group of other young police wives, "Don't you know that all cops cheat on their wives—it's part of their job description." The other wives were astonished by her remarks and judging by their facial expressions and body language, they were troubled as well. I remember thinking how obvious it was that she was bitter over a bad experience in her past, causing her to paint the whole department with one broad stroke of the brush.

Let me just digress for a brief moment to address the outburst made by that police officer's wife. The writer of the New Testament book of Hebrews says, "See to it that no one misses the grace of God and that no bitter root grows up to cause trouble and defile many" (Hebrews 12:15). There can be areas in your life where the grace of God cannot operate because of a bitter root in you. That police officer's wife, no doubt, had a bitter root that was causing trouble in her life and marriage. A bitter root will cause hardness and harshness in your life. A bitter root will rob you of joy and peace.

It is necessary to focus more on God's ability to heal you, rather than the pain that was inflicted on you by someone else. Remaining wounded hinders your ability to receive and give love. I noticed after that officer's wife made her comment, other wives slowly drifted away from her, and by the end of the night she was sitting alone.

The Bible says, "Therefore if any man [or woman] is in Christ, he is a new creature; the old things are passed away; behold, new things have come" (2 Corinthians 5:17). This is why it is so important to have a relationship with God. Later I discovered from the bitter woman's husband that she had been in long-term secular therapy in the hopes of helping with her anger and bitterness, but no one had offered her Christ. The writer of Proverbs says, "A cheerful heart does good like medicine, but a broken spirit makes one sick" (Proverbs 17:22, TLB). This woman's life was crushed; her spirit was broken and she was emotionally, physically, and spiritually sick.

There is a happy ending to this story. Because I possess an investigative nature that links up with my pastoral training, I didn't want to let this situation go unnoticed. After speaking to the woman's husband, I was able to arrange a meeting between the three of us. Over a period of time I discovered that her past experiences with her husband's infidelity had caused her to draw conclusions about life in general. It defined her value system as to what was wrong and what was right. She had determined that all police officers were a bunch of snakes that couldn't be trusted. It completely distorted her perspective on life and negatively affected her relationships, not to mention her marriage. She was hurting enough to reach a point where she wanted change in her life. She became receptive to the Bible. She allowed herself to have her mind and spirit renewed. She knew she wasn't happy. She knew that a change was needed because nothing she was doing was working. Someone once said that the definition for insanity is to do the same things over and over again, expecting a change. She knew she wasn't insane and needed to do something different. And Lord knows she did.

I was able to lead this beautiful couple through the teaching of forgiveness, redemption, and restoration. They were able to forgive one another even when it was revealed that in a fit of revenge she committed an indiscretion with a male co-worker. That was devastating to the officer, but he was able to deal with it when it happened. Both of them committed their lives to God and currently serve as Eucharistic ministers in their local church. The same woman who made the cynical statement months earlier was now able to make peace with herself, peace with her husband, and peace with her God. Don't believe that you must live with that bitter root of unforgiveness—you don't. God has other plans for you.

Getting back to healthy activities and relationships, it is also important for police officers and their spouses to acquire some healthy activities that they can enjoy on their own, so they are not strictly dependent on each other for every activity. For spouses this may be accomplished through a place of employment where social interactions are with a variety of other people on a regular basis. It may be some quality time spent with good friends or family members. One police officer told me that she takes a half a day while her husband enjoys woodworking so she can visit her nieces and nephew, building a great relationship as their aunt. The responsibility of establishing healthy activities and relationships does not rest on the shoulders of the police officer alone. It is important for a spouse to take an active role in supporting and encouraging such activities.

TEN

When a Marriage Is in Trouble

For some of you reading this book, it may appear that your marriage is near collapse. Please accept this word of encouragement that any marriage can turn around with the right care, approach, and help. If your marriage is in real disrepair, do not hesitate: Immediately make an appointment to see a pastor or marriage counselor. As you might expect from a pastor, I stress that the counselor should be a Christian counseling professional. I have had to work hard with couples in an attempt to repair their relationship after a secular counselor was through with them. So much therapy today focuses on the self, "What is going to make me happy?" Self-centeredness is not what a good marriage relationship is all about. It is about sacrificing and making your spouse a priority. Mutual submission is essential for obtaining happiness—not making yourself happy.

One time after church someone asked me how you can know when your marriage is in trouble. I said to him that a good indication a marriage is in trouble is when you go to a Hallmark card store and there isn't a single card that contains words to match your feelings. You look through the entire rack and finally settle on a card just to get out of the store. Conversely, when you are deeply in love with someone in a healthy way, every single card shouts with connection and the only problem is having too much of a selection to choose from. When I shop for a card for my wife, every card describes this beautiful sacrificial woman I am married to. The good news is that you can turn a marriage in trouble around and make it healthy and vibrant. Remember, when you hear the lyrics of the Righteous Brothers tune in your head, "You've lost that loving feeling," it's time to think about practicing sacrificial love.

Marriages in trouble do not happen overnight. The death of a marriage is a slow and painful process that can be prevented. When someone comes into my office and tells me that his spouse is acting funny all of a sudden, it doesn't take very long to figure out that the all of a sudden wasn't so sudden after all. The fire in a marriage doesn't suddenly go out—it slowly burns down. And you need to be patient during the rebuilding process. As already stated, your marriage didn't get into trouble overnight—and neither will it repair itself overnight. You will have to invest the time, prayer, and patience in nurturing it back to life.

Perhaps you were not prepared for the idiosyncrasies of married life. I am amazed at the number of couples I initially counsel who say they received no premarital counseling before their wedding day. I believe pastors and priests who are more concerned with the insignificant details than coaching and mentoring young couples in what a healthy marriage should look like, are doing a tremendous disservice to the couple and our culture as a whole. If by chance you are considering getting married and the pastor who is marrying you does not sufficiently counsel you, ask the pastor why. And if that is not part of his or her routine, find another pastor.

What about the Spouse's End of the Bargain?

Today, secular standards have been applied to the institution of marriage and they simply are not working. A 50 percent or less success rate would be a failing grade in any respectable learning institution—so why is it not considered a failing grade within the institution of marriage? Unfortunately, little biblical instruction is given to either husband or wife in how to fulfill each of their roles. And sadly, a good part of the church has fallen asleep in its responsibility to provide this instruction. Words like submission, sacrifice, and unconditional love do not appear on the politically-correct radar screen—so they are rarely used or completely ignored in many of our nation's pulpits.

In order for marriage to work, we need to know, understand, and respect our space. Respect literally means "to again look at." A lot of marriages that are failing or have lost their passion will require that the husband and wife take another look at each other and make every effort to really get to know one another. About a year ago I officiated a wedding of a city police officer whose father-in-law was a retired DEA investigator. Several months after the wedding I bumped into the officer in our local mall. He asked if I would be willing to reach out to his father-in-law who was struggling in his marriage of over forty years. I eventually met with this retired federal cop and heard something I had heard many times before. After all his years of marriage—raising the kids, working long hours on the job, going to schools and training—he was now retired and had discovered that he really didn't know the woman he had been married to for over forty years. What a pity that two persons could live together for so long and not really know each other. You see, respect means "to again look at" and look at and look at and look at. I think you get the picture.

Good and open communication is the key to accomplishing this level of respect and support in a marriage. Getting to know each other is a huge building block in the foundation of a successful marriage. This was sadly missing for over forty years in the retired DEA investigator's marriage. Don't wake up one morning with the kids all grown and gone, wondering who that person is sleeping next to you.

Once a police officer's wife said to me, "Pastor, on the job my husband is Mr. Law and Order where everyone has to snap to his command. Yeah, when he puts on that uniform he is a knight in shining armor. But when he gets home I have to give him a reality check that he is just plain old Fred, my husband." In some ways I thought what she said was comical—however, when you think about it, it is really a sad commentary. Listen to her words, do they sound very encouraging? Do they convey any level of respect? Of course, Fred shouldn't have a swelled head, either. But what would be wrong with her letting Fred know that she was proud of him and what he does on the job? My wife, bless her heart, has always let me know that I am the greatest man in her life. She has always been my greatest encourager and fan. I have not always deserved that title or place of endearment—but that is exactly how she makes me feel.

Although I am more often disappointed by the way a male police officer treats his wife, I am regularly discouraged by the way police wives act toward their husbands. Ruth Graham, wife of evangelist Billy Graham, married for over sixty years, once said, "It is God's job to keep him humble; it is my job to love him."[14] I believe a strong glue that has helped keep my marriage together over the years has been my wife offering encouragement, respect, and unconditional love even when she didn't feel like giving it. She's my greatest supporter, helper, and friend.

A Wedding Day Must Always Be Cherished and Remembered

Occasionally while I am in my church study I will take a telephone call, usually from a young lady, asking, "Do you do weddings?" Sort of like, "Do you do oil changes?" Then comes the next question, "How much do you charge for a wedding?" To which I answer, "Well, for beginners, a minimum of eight to ten premarital counseling sessions where you and your fiancée will deal with topics and issues like finances and budgets, communication, human sexuality, extended family issues, spirituality, biblical mandates for marriage..." I'll either hear a click on the other end or a comment like, "Oh, me and Freddie were looking at getting married two weeks from Saturday. You see, we already have the reception hall and photographer, but we don't have a minister yet."

A wedding is more than getting something done so you can get to the reception hall. It is a sacred covenant between the couple getting married and God. When a minister officiates a wedding, that wedding becomes a religious ceremony where a life-long covenant occurs and not just a legal procedure like closing on a house. A covenant is not some legal contract.

When I was working as a lieutenant assigned to Midtown Manhattan, a very despondent fellow lieutenant came to me while we were working a labor strike at Con Edison. This lieutenant lamented to me how his fiancée walked out on him earlier in the day. I asked what precipitated her leaving, knowing he was scheduled to marry soon. Then he told me the story.

He had arranged for her to meet him at his lawyer's office to review and sign a prenuptial agreement. She thought they were going to review documents pertaining to a house they were going to purchase and live in after their honeymoon. The legal document he wanted her to sign was drawn up to read that in the event they divorced, she would not be entitled to his police pension. She was absolutely shocked and devastated upon reading the contents of the document she was asked to sign.

With tears streaming down her cheeks, she stood up and said to this dumbfounded lieutenant, "If you don't think this marriage will work and there is a possibility for divorce before we even enter into union with each other—I'd rather not marry. Goodbye, Gene, and good luck with your life." Gene said to me, "Chuck, was I wrong? I'm only trying to protect a pension that I shed a lot of blood, sweat, and tears for." Unfortunately, I didn't see it the same way. You see, in the eyes of Gene's fiancée, it wasn't about dividing up property and assets. For her, marriage was a covenant with a "no escape clause" written in. The only escape clause is "until death do us part," and for her, rightfully so, the marriage covenant is binding. It is about keeping your end of the deal and not trying to find a loophole to get out of it.

More Than Mere Words

The various wedding ceremonies followed by Christian denominations contain beautiful wording and meaning. The United Methodist Hymnal contains the service of marriage, which the denomination considers a true service of worship and not merely a ritual that gets the couple to their reception hall and the honeymoon that follows. Marriage is proclaimed as a sacred covenant reflecting Christ's own covenant with the church. It is made clear in our hymnal text that even the people gathered to witness the ceremony are not just friends, family, and passive witnesses—but rather an active congregation.

One of the very first announcements a minister makes to the bride and groom and gathered congregation is that everyone is "gathered before God" and throughout the service God is a witness to and participant in the union. In the "Declaration of Intention," both the bride and groom are asked: "Will you live together in holy marriage? Will you love, comfort, honor and keep your partner, in sickness and health and forsaking all others, be faithful to him or her as long as you both shall live?"[15] Consider those words for a moment: love, comfort, honor, and keep. When we love someone, we display affection, tenderness, admiration, warmth, devotion, and unselfish loyalty. When we comfort someone, we support and console him or her in times of trouble. When we honor someone, we show him or her respect. When we keep another, we protect and remain faithful and walk alongside to help fulfill the other.

Remember Lenny? Although he said these words at the altar on his wedding day, they were empty and without conviction. This is why it is so important to prepare for marriage in a way that has nothing to do with details.

How long does one maintain such a relationship as described above? Until the first problem arises? Does such a declaration run out over time? The obvious answer is no. Part of the declaration states that "in sickness and in health, and forsaking all others, be faithful as long as you live."[16] This is a declaration made before God and all the gathered company before a single vow is made. But I meet many police officers who talk like the life-long commitment they made on their wedding day was more like a life sentence. How I like to approach the life-long commitment I made to my wife is to take each day at a time. I try to approach my marriage with freshness each day and to make a daily commitment to be the very best husband I can be for the next 24 hours. What that helps me to do is focus on a short span of time that I can usually handle well.

I begin each day with a prayer that includes, among other petitions, asking God to help me to hand over my life to his control throughout the day. I request His assistance in helping me place my wife's needs ahead of my own and to be sacrificial in my marital relationship. When you take an approach at marriage like that, the whole notion of a life-long commitment becomes much more manageable. The Psalmist writes, "Commit everything you do to the Lord. Trust him to help you do it, and he will" (Psalm 37:4 TLB).

Let's take a look at what vows are actually exchanged during a wedding ceremony. Although some couples write their own vows quoting all kinds of interesting poetry and song lyrics—in order for me to officiate a wedding, the vows must contain the basic covenantal language that lends spiritual significance. In my tradition the vows are as follows:

"In the name of God, I, [Name], take you, [Name], to be my wife (or husband), to have and to hold from this day forward, for better, for worse, for richer, for poorer, in sickness and in health, to love and to cherish, until we are parted by death. This is my solemn vow."[17]

Listen to the incredible beauty and significance of the words: to have and to hold, in good times and in bad times, regardless of finances (which is a leading cause for separations and divorce), whether my partner is healthy or struggling with illness, and to always love and cherish. Webster's Dictionary defines the word cherish as, "To hold dear; feel or show affection; to keep or cultivate with care and affection; to nurture; to entertain or harbor in the mind deeply and resolutely."

I have been married for a very long time, yet I consider these vows on a regular basis. My wife and I have been through some very difficult times with serious physical illnesses, financially lean moments, and some interesting disagreements. Nevertheless, we have resolved to take our vows seriously and to remember that they were made for life. I truly believe I love my wife more today than any other time before.

There is a place in the service where the rings are blessed and it is mentioned that each ring is an "outward and visible sign of an inward and spiritual grace, signifying to us the union between Jesus Christ and his church." Just as Jesus' relationship with the church is unbroken, so is the ring we slip on the finger of our future spouse. The words shared by both bride and groom as they exchange their wedding rings are equally as important and beautiful:

"[Name], I give you this ring as a sign of my vow, and with all that I am, and all that I have, I honor you; in the name of the Father, and the Son, and the Holy Spirit."

Then the minister offers the declaration of marriage. As the new husband and wife join hands, the pastor addresses the couple with these words:

"You have declared your consent and vows before God and this congregation. May God confirm your covenant and fill you both with grace."

The minister then proclaims to the entire congregation:

"Now that [Name] and [Name] have given themselves to each other by solemn vows, with the joining of hands, and the giving and receiving of rings, I announce to you that they are husband and wife; in the name of the Father, and the Son, and of the Holy Spirit. Those whom God has joined together, let no one put asunder."

Often times there is a unity candle lit during the service when the bride and groom receive a lighted flame from two separate candles and using the lighter candles in their possession, at the same time they light a large unity candle, signifying two becoming one—two individuals becoming one—two families uniting together.

The covenantal words spoken by a couple pledging their vows for marriage are more than mere words. They make a promise to each other and to God to be loyal. When a couple keeps those promises, they can overcome any obstacle they may face in this life.

Divorce Is Not the Only Option

Divorce rates amongst police are twice as high as in other occupations. There are clear reasons for this—but it doesn't have to be that way. It is my prayer that if you are reading this book and considering a divorce, you will reconsider and try to work things out. God gave us the institution of marriage and it is very close to his heart.

From the very beginning of creation, God presented marriage as His gift to humanity. Adam and Eve were created perfect for each other.[18] Marriage was not just for convenience to save on our taxes, nor was it brought about by any culture. Marriage was established by God, and He said it was good.

Often times, but not always, people considering divorce come from families who experienced divorce. Judith Wallerstein conducted a 25 year study of the effects of divorce, and discovered "men and women from divorced families live in fear that they will repeat their parents' history, hardly daring to hope that they can do better....As children grow up and choose partners of their own, they lack this central image of the intact marriage. In its place they confront a void that threatens to swallow them whole....Their conclusion is simple.... Failure is inevitable."[19] But failure is not inevitable.

We are living in a day when divorce not only doesn't have a social stigma like it did in the past, but divorce has become a normal and expected occurrence done with convenience and little effort. And so, for convenience, but at a painful cost, divorce becomes an easy "bail out" mechanism that only perpetuates the fulfillment of the false prophecy a couple may have held when entering the relationship. The officers that I have written about in previous chapters had fallen victim to this lie. So rather than getting caught in a vicious cycle of divorce because we witnessed it in our families growing up or it has become a popular societal norm—look for ways to reconcile and restore your relationship, rather than abandoning it.

I would be remiss if I didn't add that there are some situations that require an individual to leave the home and possibly seek legal separation that may ultimately lead to a divorce. While Christianity does not support divorce, it also does not want God's children to be abused. I have walked into apartments and homes where the wife was beaten to a pulp by some big, cowardly drunk for a husband. There is no way I would recommend a wife to remain in that home and try to work things out from the inside. As God's creation we were never created to remain in an ongoing abusive relationship. This would hold true for physical, emotional, verbal, and/or sexual abuse of the children in the house.

I have worked with couples who have found themselves in an abusive marital relationship that was eventually healed because the abuser experienced conversion, earnestly sought healing, and by the grace of God changed his ways. We were not created by God to be abused or to be an abuser—and that must be understood by both parties. It has been my experience that once the hitting starts by either the wife or husband, it becomes easier the next time. Stop it the first time.

If by chance you are dealing with violence on the job that has spilled over into your marriage and home where you are now verbally and/or physically abusing your spouse—you need to repent immediately, seek forgiveness from your spouse, and seek help from your chaplain, minister, or counseling professional in dealing with your aggressive behavior. It is never acceptable or excusable. The Bible says, "If we confess our sins, he is faithful and just and will forgive us our sins and purify us from all unrighteousness" (1 John 1:9). Be big enough to admit that what you did was wrong and seek God's help so as to never do it again.

Spouses Have an Obligation to Be Proactive, Not Just Reactive

It is important for a police officer's spouse to know as much about his or her spouse's profession as possible. You should not remain in the dark or in ignorance about what the life of a police officer entails. A realistic picture of what is involved in the daily routine of a police officer will help a spouse to better understand their husband or wife and increase the effectiveness of their communication. The old attitude of "What he does at work stays at work—when he's home, he's home" is not a good position to take as a spouse of a police officer. Of course it is not necessary to share every nitty-gritty detail of the police life, but some basic understanding of the job should be known.

If your husband or wife's department offers a Citizen's Police Academy program, enroll and learn more about the inner working of the agency. If the department doesn't offer such program, write a letter to the chief of the department and request one be established. Sign up for a ride-along so you can get a front line experience of the police officer's life. All of these measures will only serve to enlighten you as a spouse of a cop. I wish more departments would run an evening orientation class for spouses and families of police officers. Seasoned officers and administrators could be available to answer questions and concerns of the family members of a newly appointed officer. Perhaps spouses of veteran officers could participate in the discussions to serve as coaches or mentors for rookie spouses. The police family is important enough for a department to invest the time and resources in such an educational program. I have always known that a cop who is happy at home is a cop who is happy and effective on the job.

ELEVEN

The Root of Financial Problems

Police families who financially overextend themselves are not unique. Nevertheless, financial debt is one of the most common causes of major stress in the life of a police officer. Banks and other lending institutions love to make credit available to cops knowing that for the most part police departments keep a tight rein on their employees.

Cops regularly work second jobs or as many overtime details as possible to increase their income. That may be a noble endeavor, but I have found it is not always necessary. One police officer told me how strapped for cash he was and how it was causing a real strain on his marriage, so I agreed to pay the couple a visit at their home to discuss ways they could navigate through their problems. As I pulled up to their house the first thing I noticed were the two cars that were parked in their driveway. There was a brand new 4x4, fully-loaded pickup truck and a $30,000 SUV parked next to it. Once I entered the house, I observed from the foyer a large-screen television with surround sound in the family room. Believe me, the list goes on. They weren't strapped for cash—they were tied to an obsession for big ticket items, with nothing but credit to pay for them. They had the taste of Donald Trump with the checkbook of Mother Teresa.

I cannot claim to be a qualified financial planner or debt counselor, but I am a pastor of a young and growing congregation and an ex-cop who has, for the most part, practiced good stewardship my entire life. Honestly, I can make such a statement as a result of having watched my parents never live a lifestyle that was above their means. That had a great influence on my life. With the credit scores my wife and I have—every lending institution and credit card company is always trying to throw credit our way.

Let me begin by saying something encouraging to you—if you are presently in debt, you can get out of the jam you are in—but, it is going to involve some tough choices, good discipline and hard work. There are no easy solutions other than a rich uncle leaving you a large inheritance—and even then, without making those difficult decisions, practicing good discipline and hard work, you'd go through that inheritance like a buzz saw and be in trouble all over again.

I encounter police officers all the time that can't even make the minimum payment on their credit card bills—not to mention the family car that needs new brakes and the kids who need braces. We all know the trouble signs that you are drowning in debt:

- Carrying a balance on your credit card and making minimum payments while continuing to charge.
- Noticing a pattern of past due notices piling up.
- Creditors or collection agencies writing you notice after notice or regularly calling your home causing you to screen all your calls.

This is not the way for you to live your life. Being in that kind of debt makes you a prisoner or the property of someone else. You are not your own—you're in bondage. And it is a debilitating condition for anyone to be in. The good news is that you can get out from under that mess. But let me immediately dismiss some foolish assumptions or even fantasies on the part of individuals. If you are like some members of my extended family, you may be thinking that you will one day be standing before the flashes of news cameras while accepting the state's jumbo mega supernatural extravaganza lottery prize. There you would be, your pearly whites gleaming in the lights, accepting that giant cardboard check from the lottery commissioner. Hello. Wake Up. It is just a dream. Get real—it just ain't gonna happen. As far as that rich uncle—he's not out there, either. Thinking your creditors are going to find out what a great guy you are and knowing you are a little strapped for cash, they'll just forgive your loans? Don't think so. Listen, you were the guy who was hoping that when Y2K came that all of the computers would be wiped out along with your credit records—and that didn't happen either, did it?

Reality Check

It is not a pleasant place to be when you are in a financial crisis, when there are bills to be paid and no cash to pay them. But you really have to sit down and evaluate why you are in this present crisis. Before I continue any further, I must mention that not all financial problems are caused by overspending—sometimes unpredictable emergencies arise that could not have been prevented—a medical emergency, an original good investment that went bad, or a business that failed. Nevertheless, most every cop I counsel who is experiencing a financial crisis has gotten there due to overspending, over-extending, and out-of-control credit accessing.

You must learn how to buy what you can afford and not necessarily what you want. Let's just face it—we live in a plastic happy culture where instant gratification is driving the train. The system is set up for failure. Before you know it, you're in trouble. Living with the notion that if you just have that one more "thing" you will be happy, is a lie. That new car will make you happy for a season, but after a couple of dings and a bad winter, it becomes just a car—but a car with a $600 payment attached to it every month. The only things that we need are food, water, healthcare, and shelter—everything else is a luxury. You won't die without that MP3 player or wide screen TV. I recently waited several months before I purchased my MP3 player because I would not purchase it until I was able to pay for it. As a result of my delayed gratification, I now own my iPod and not some credit card company owning me. St. Paul said, "I have learned to be content whatever the circumstances" (Philippians 4:11). We really must learn how to be content with what we already have.

So What Do You Do Now?

I didn't have to tell you that you were in financial trouble—you already knew that. So what do you do now to get out of it? There are a number of things you can do. So your first course of action is to pray; no prayer is a wasted prayer. In your prayers, ask God to point out areas and attitudes in your life that need to be changed and to provide you with the necessary help to make those changes. Remember that God is very much concerned about your well-being. He loves you and wants the very best for you—but he also loves you so much that he doesn't want to leave you the same way you are. He doesn't want to leave you practicing bad habits that will continue to get you in trouble.

As you pray, you must divorce yourself from a modern notion that everything that happens in life has a quick fix to it. You can get your oil changed in less than eight minutes. We have drive-thru pharmacies, banks, and eateries. There is even a drive-thru funeral home in Florida where you can view the deceased from a window without leaving your car.

You might want to beware of the pitfalls set up by shrewd retailers and creditors. For instance, blow-out sales at the mall are only a sale if you need an item and you can afford it—otherwise it is not a sale, but added debt. Also, bonus points or air miles provided by credit card companies may be an added benefit to using your credit card, but it can also be a lure into the spider's web of debt. Be careful that you do not justify frequent spending by rationalizing that every purchase gets you that much closer to a great getaway to paradise. Remember, it usually takes 40,000 air miles to earn you a single domestic flight plane ticket. If you are earning one mile for every dollar spent—you will have to charge $40,000 to earn one ticket. Depending on the time of the year, you could purchase the same ticket to Orlando for under $200. Don't fall into the air miles trap of unnecessary spending. On the other hand, I automatically pay all my required bills like insurance payments, utilities, telephone, broadband service, etc., by credit card. I have to pay these monthly bills anyway, so why not pay them and accumulate air miles as well? However, I make certain to pay the total balance of the credit card each month. It costs me nothing extra and racks up the air miles. That is a wise use of the bonus or air miles credit card. You also want to be very cautious when walking through the doors of so-called membership discount retailers like Sam's Club or Costco. These are great places if you are purchasing rations for the 82nd Airborne Division. No doubt there are items that you can purchase that will save you dollars—but what usually happens is you begin filling up one or two carts with items you never intended to purchase. From a list of cereal, juice, and dishwasher detergent—you can end up walking out of the store with a portable stereo, air compressor, and 30 pounds of junk food. Be intentional with a prepared shopping list if you are going to walk into a large warehouse retailer or the local grocery store. Remain focused on your shopping list and only buy what you need.

Put plain and simple, if you want to get out of debt, you have to change your way of thinking and your way of living. Let's be honest, if you are driving that new fancy car, living in a house that is too much for your income, and buying all the gadgets—you are the owner of nothing, but rather you are a renter of a lifestyle. It is all on lease just like when you rent or lease a car on vacation. You are driving it, but it's not yours. If you want the burden of debt lifted off of your shoulders you will have to start thinking smart, begin to make good choices, and practice a disciplined way of life when it comes to spending. A great way to do that is to immediately stop borrowing. Yes, stop borrowing beginning today and don't put it off. Do not make a single purchase for something that you are unable to pay cash for. No excuses—just cease and desist. Then sit down and make a list of all your debt and what interest rates you are paying on each line of debt. Get a realistic picture of what your income is and what you are expected to pay out each month. If there is too much month left at the end of your paycheck—immediate action is necessary. By discontinuing your borrowing (which means no future spending by using credit rather than your own money), you are now in a position to begin paying down your outstanding credit card balances. With the proper assistance you can consolidate all your debt into one single loan at a cumulative lesser interest rate requiring you to make a single payment each month at a lower out of pocket expense. Next, cut up all your credit cards and once they are paid off cancel them immediately. You can hold on to one major credit card for emergencies, but as one financial planner suggests, consider placing the card in a plastic container filled with water and freeze it in your freezer. This way, whenever you are tempted to make a purchase, your card will not be immediately accessible and you will first have to defrost the container to get to the card. Also, make certain that the one credit card you do maintain has the best available interest rate and no annual fee. Get in the habit of making purchases with cash, personal check, or a debit card that works off of what you actually have in your checking account. By doing so you will most likely buy less and steer away from items you cannot afford.

Getting the Right Help to Make It Happen

Seek out the help of a financial advisor. You may be thinking, how can I afford the services of a financial advisor when I'm already broke? You cannot afford not to seek out help—but it may not cost you anything but your time and honest effort. Speak with your chaplain or pastor and ask them for help. They are often able to put you in touch with a church member who has expertise in the area of finance management and who can help you pro bono or as part of his or her

Christian service.

In seeking help, be honest with yourself, with God, and with the person helping you. Provide the helper with all the facts and figures, just as they are, so you can develop a realistic picture of your situation and a realistic approach to solving the problem. You can be on the road to recovery today—but only you can make that decision.

One of the crucial things a financial counselor will help you with is the establishing of a budget. Having a budget is not optional—it is essential. You will also be helped in prioritizing your debt according to balances and interest rates and how far you are in arrears on each account. The counselor will walk you through the process of debt consolidation I mentioned earlier. It may be recommended that you downsize in certain areas of your lifestyle. You may need to move into a smaller house or drive a more inexpensive vehicle or brown bag it at work. It may mean delaying or postponing that trip to Disney World.

There are far too many topics concerning finances that cannot be sufficiently covered in a book of this nature. Help with issues like good long-term investing and smart insurance purchasing can be obtained through a plethora of self-help books on the market as well as through your financial counselor. The bottom line and final note for this section is the urgency that you and your spouse must learn early on to live within your means.

TWELVE

Look out for Your Kids

"Fathers, do not embitter your children, or they will become discouraged" (Colossians 3:21).

It was a cold night outside the famous Madison Square Garden where my Tactical Unit was assigned as an outside security detail during a rock concert. Summoned by Garden security guards to one of the entranceways, we were directed to a 17-year-old youth who was obviously drunk and disorderly. When I asked him to leave, he greeted me with a string of obscenities. I then grabbed him by his left arm and with his free hand he punched me in the side of the head. Within seconds he was subdued, handcuffed, and escorted to a police van for transportation to the station.

When we arrived at the precinct, he threatened to have my badge taken away because his father was a police lieutenant. After making his allowed phone calls, about 45 minutes later, his father arrived at the station house. He called me aside and asked me to let his son go. When I informed him that his son punched me in the head and I was charging him with felony assault, the father acted very similarly to his son. He became threatening, spewing obscenities, until the desk lieutenant warned him that if he didn't calm down, he would be joining his son in the detention room. What was clearly evident to me was that the old adage, "Like father, like son" was true in this case.

I eventually calmed the boy down, bought him something to eat and drink, and he shared with me that he was surprised that the "old man" even came down to the precinct. He said that his father was rarely home and when he was, it was almost impossible for anyone to have peace in the house. He never remembered his father attending a sporting event or even visiting his school—always using "the job" as his excuse for not being more involved. His father often manhandled him and his older brother as if they were street criminals. His brother eventually dropped out of high school and joined the army. The boy further stated that his father was rude to his mother and suspected that he was also physically abusive with her when he wasn't around. I asked him, "Son, why did you punch me?" He replied, "I hate my father, and my father is a cop, and hitting you in some strange way gave me the opportunity of hitting him without facing him. You were my father standing there."

You see, this really wasn't a bad kid. He was just a kid who had absolutely no positive relationship with his father. Dr. Henry Cloud states, "Relationship is central not only to the order of the universe God has created, but also to parenting. You can't construct character in a child without a deep relationship with parents."[20] Children need a relationship with their mom and dad. They need to be loved and affirmed. They need to know that they are more important than the job. We need to live our lives by presenting them with a positive example. We need to provide them with quality time. Deuteronomy 6:20 says that fathers ought to teach their children the deeper meanings of God and faith. St. Paul was reminded of Timothy's sincere faith because he received it from his mother and grandmother (2 Timothy 1:5).

Faith and Christian values are not obtained through osmosis, but rather are taught by parents. Deuteronomy 4:10 instructs us to teach our children and our children's children the ways of the Lord. Two chapters later, Moses instructs us as parents "Love the Lord your God with all your heart and with all your soul and with all your strength. These commandments that I give you today are to be upon your hearts. Impress them on your children. Talk about them when you sit at home and when you walk along the road, when you lie down and when you get up" (Deuteronomy 6:4-7).

Solomon commands us fathers to tell our children, "My [child], keep your father's commands and do not forsake your mother's teaching. Bind them upon your heart forever; fasten them around your neck. When you walk, they will guide you; when you sleep, they will watch over you; when you awake, they will speak to you. For these commands are a lamp, this teaching is a light, and the corrections of discipline are the way to life, keeping you from the immoral" (Proverbs 6:20-23). Do you think that boy would have punched me that night

78

had his father followed the instructions found in the Bible?

That cop's kid saw "dad" and "work" as being synonymous. His home was more like a prison than a place of security. When his dad was home everyone had to walk around on eggshells. No matter how tough the job may get—your family doesn't deserve to live like that. Be positive. Be an encourager. Be available. Reevaluate your priorities and make sure your family is placed high on the list. Create an environment where you are truly missed when you are not home and sincerely appreciated when you are.

Recently, a police officer's wife told me, "Since my husband switched from midnights to the 4 p.m. to midnight shift, there is peace in our house and lives. My kids said that it is so nice not to have daddy home in the evenings. Pastor, the tension is out of the house—we have a sense of freedom. We can move about like a family again. I know it's wrong, but it's true." This particular police officer was a tyrant in his home. The voice his family was most familiar with was a voice that was always yelling. He was usually grumpy, moody, and irritable. Until he left for work he remained planted on the couch, watching TV while his wife sat in the kitchen and his kids stayed in their rooms. Now working the 4-12 shift, the wife, because she worked during the day, only saw him on his days off and the kids for a half hour before he left for work. Sadly, they were all happy with the arrangement. This was a dysfunctional family on the road to long-term disaster.

Erma Bombeck, someone with a great take on life, once wrote, "When the good Lord was creating fathers he started with a tall frame. And a female angel nearby said, 'What kind of father is that? If you're going to make children so close to the ground, why have you put fathers up so high? He won't be able to shoot marbles without kneeling, tuck a child in bed without bending, or even kiss a child without a lot of stooping.' And God smiled and said, 'Yes, but if I make him child-size, who would children have to look up to?'

"And when God made a father's hands, they were large and sinewy. And the angel shook her head sadly and said, 'Do you know what you're doing? Large hands are clumsy. They can't manage diaper pins, small buttons, or rubber bands on pony tails, or even remove splinters caused by baseball bats.' And God smiled and said, 'I know, but they're large enough to hold everything a small boy empties from his pockets at the end of a day...yet small enough to cup a child's face.'

"God worked throughout the night, giving the father few words,

79

but a firm authoritative voice; eyes that saw everything, but remained calm and tolerant. Finally, almost as an afterthought, he added tears. Then he turned to the angel and said, 'Now, are you satisfied that he can love as much as a mother?' The angel was quiet."[21]

You see, God has provided fathers, even fathers who are cops, with the capacity and tool box to be a loving and caring dad. I know your job is tough—I've been there, I got the T-shirt. I know you deal with situations few people understand. But with God's help, you can maintain the right perspective on life and not make your family pay for something they don't deserve.

THIRTEEN

A Cop's Attitude

"Good attitudes among players do not guarantee a team's success, but bad attitudes guarantee its failure."[22]
—*John Maxwell*

Don't judge a book by its cover. Proper protocol within the New York Police Department is for arresting officers to stop at the desk lieutenant to log in his or her prisoner. However, rarely was this practiced when squad detectives made a collar. On one particular shift I was both the desk lieutenant and overall precinct supervisor, when two detectives walked past the desk with a prisoner who looked more like a cop than a criminal. As they walked by one of the detectives glanced in my direction and said, "One under arrest, lieu." Little did I know that the "one under" was Mickey Featherstone.

The infamous Mickey Featherstone was an absolute legend in Hell's Kitchen—especially amongst police officers assigned to the Westside precincts. Mickey was on mental disability as a Vietnam veteran who served with the 5th Special Forces in the Macon Delta. By the time Mickey crossed my path he had already committed numerous homicides and had a well-deserved reputation as a guy you wouldn't want to even glance at in the wrong way. He had a hair-trigger temper that could easily erupt into gunfire and death.

Mickey Featherstone was a 5'9", 138-pound tough Irish kid who could easily be mistaken as a choir boy at the local Catholic parish. But his youthful good looks, sandy blonde hair, and unassuming small build was deceiving. Just months after returning home from Vietnam, Mickey was sitting in the Leprechaun Bar on 9th Avenue and West 44th Street drinking a beer and minding his own business, when a 6'1", 200-pound southern truck driver barked at him, "What are you looking at, punk?" Calm, cool, and collected, Mickey told the bigger man to get lost. The drunken truck driver challenged Mickey to step outside and began to describe all the things he would do to the smaller opponent. Mickey put down his beer, stepped outside and before the challenger could throw his first punch, Mickey shot him twice in the chest with a .25 caliber automatic. While the man lay dying on the cold Manhattan sidewalk—witnesses said that Mickey stepped over the body and casually walked down the street.

Featherstone had committed three homicides before his 21st birthday and developed his reputation on the streets of Hell's Kitchen, an area covering West 34th Street to West 59th Street and 8th Avenue to the Hudson River. Though historically populated by Irish, it slowly became a melting pot of all kinds of nationalities. This community raised up the likes of the actor James Cagney, politicians, cops, priests, and some of the most notorious gangsters.

Young Mickey Featherstone worked his way up through the ranks of the Westside Irish crime family, eventually becoming the number two man behind the boss, Jimmy Coonan. Although Featherstone and his cronies didn't embrace the name, cops on the West side dubbed them, "The Westies." The Westies had their tentacles in every aspect of criminal activity: loan sharking, protection, drugs, extortion, gambling, counterfeiting, and their number one specialty, murder for hire. Their modus operandi was to use small caliber weapons equipped with silencers, shoot their victim, and then dismember the body. Hit victim's body parts were then carried off in several plastic bags and either dumped in the East River off of Ward's Island or buried along the old New York Central Railway tracks between 10th and 11th Avenues.

It is quite incredible how Mickey worked his way in and out of jams by doing short prison sentences or stays at the hospital for the insane. Whenever a Westie crime went down, not a soul on the Westside was a witness. When asked, the response was always the same, "I ain't seen nothing.'"

It was rumored, and I believe eventually substantiated, that Mickey Featherstone's gang joined forces with Paul Castalano's Mafia crime family which only added to him being virtually untouchable. Just as a side note, I was working Manhattan South Borough Headquarters the night Paul "Big Paulie" Castalano, the *capo di tutti capi* and his bodyguard, Thomas Bilotti, were gunned down outside Sparks Steak

House by enforcers from John Gotti's crime family.

While the detectives settled in their modern day desperado who was brought in for allegedly gunning down a construction worker on 34th Street in broad daylight, I reminisced about my first direct involvement with The Westies gang. The time was three years earlier when I was the evening plainclothes anti-crime sergeant in the busiest command in the city—the Midtown South Precinct.

Normally, as the supervisor, I would patrol with two officers assigned to the unit. This provided me with the opportunity to spend time with my subordinates, get to know them and their work habits. Our anti-crime unit had several Yellow Cabs assigned to us so as to blend into the traffic flow of Midtown Manhattan without raising suspicion on the part of the criminal element.

The Midtown South Anti-Crime Unit was made up of 27 police officers and two sergeants. I worked the evening shift of 5 p.m. to 1 a.m. while my counterpart, Sergeant Levine, worked the day shift. Levine specialized in truck hijackings and other forms of theft while my platoon focused primarily on robberies, burglaries, and other serious felonies. The officers assigned to the unit were the very best street cops and could smell out a felon within five city blocks. They averaged some 300 felony arrests each month.

That particular evening I was fully expecting to go out on the streets of Manhattan looking for nocturnal bad guys traveling in from the Bronx and Brooklyn, just like a regular job, looking for victims to rob. After completing some paperwork, I joined up with Officers Carmichael and Sullivan. Stopping at the Market Diner on West 43rd Street and 11th Avenue, a favorite hangout for the Westies, Sullivan went inside to pick up coffee. Carmichael and I started to discuss the potential 1982 baseball season when a call came over our radio reporting a shooting in the parking lot at Pier 92 on West 57th Street and 11th Avenue. At the time it was confirmed that three men were shot and one female was taken against her will. The armed suspect, a white male, driving a van had fled south. We were 14 blocks south of the scene of the shooting and in the direct path of the suspect's escape route if he continued south. There was a strong likelihood of his passing us any moment. Advising Sullivan of what was going down, he threw the cups of coffee in the street and jumped in the cab.

It couldn't have been timed any better when a white van with dark stripes sped past us. The chase was on. Here was a yellow taxi cab chasing a white van through the streets of Manhattan. The traffic on the radio was so intense that we could not get through to the dispatcher. With Sullivan and me in the back seat of this Checker cab and Carmichael at the wheel, it felt as if we were on a theme park ride bouncing over pot holes and making turns on two wheels. This was our guy and we knew it. After several blocks he managed to squeeze through the congested traffic and get away. Carmichael punched the steering wheel as we frantically weaved in and out of streets hoping to pick up the trail again—but he was long gone. The shooting was a classic Westie contract killing that went bad.

Early the next morning, the body of the abducted woman was discovered by a guy walking his dog through an alley on Franklin Place between White and Franklin Streets, near Broadway. Her name was Margaret Barbera, a 38-year-old bookkeeper who had plead guilty to Federal conspiracy charges involving fraud in connection with her boss, who was in jail and who put the contract out on her and one other female employee. Everyone knew that if a contract killing was needed you could always count on the Westies. One month prior to Ms. Barbera's murder, the same hit man abducted the other female witness, Jenny Soo Chin, outside of Ms. Barbera's Ridgewood, Queens apartment and she was never to be seen again. Remember that the Westies specialized in murder and dismemberment.

On the night we lost our suspect, he had been waiting next to Ms. Barbera's car for an opportunity to abduct her. As the abduction took place, she screamed, drawing the attention of three innocent CBS workers who were walking to their car. As they rallied to her assistance, the suspect shot the woman behind the ear with a .22 caliber handgun equipped with silencer, a classic Westie shooting, and dumped her body by the side door of the van. Realizing there were witnesses, he methodically chased down all three men, shooting them in the head. All three died instantly. A fourth witness managed to go undetected and was able to call the police.

A thorough investigation under the direction of Chief of Detectives, James T. Sullivan, came up with a long-time citizen of Hell's Kitchen, Donald Nash, who was arrested and charged with four counts of murder and one count of conspiracy to murder. Thirteen months after the night of the original shooting, Donald Nash was found guilty of all charges and sent to prison for the rest of his life.

I snapped out of my daydreaming as the phone rang on the front desk with a reporter wanting to know if we had Mickey Featherstone in custody. Members of the New York press were just as good as any detective on the force. They had a sixth sense for snooping out information that would put the C.I.A. to shame. As usual, I told him to call the Current Situations Desk at Police Headquarters for any information.

Jimmy Delaney was a good kid who was out of the police academy about a year. His hat appeared to be a half-size too big so it always looked like it rested over his eyes pushing down his ears. He was assigned to Station House security, helping relieve inside workers for lunch, directing people at the door, and using an out-of-service R.M.P. (radio motor patrol) cruiser to make coffee runs to the diner.

That day he went up to the detective squad to ask if anyone wanted something from the diner. Sitting on a chair, with his right wrist handcuffed to a rail, was Mickey Featherstone. He certainly did not give the appearance of a guy who could take your life and eat a pastrami sandwich while sitting on your chest. Delaney yelled into the squad room, "You guys want anything from the diner? I'm making a run!" Mickey Featherstone looked up and said, "Hey, can you get me a cup of coffee?" Delaney kicked Featherstone's outstretched legs and basically told him to go where the sun don't shine.

After Delaney came downstairs to the desk, he said to me and the sergeant, "What an a**hole upstairs," and shared that he had taught the guy in custody a lesson on how to speak to a cop. When we told Delaney who that guy attached to the handcuffs was—it looked like all the life drained out of his face as he turned a bright red and then pale white. I said, "Delaney, you just kicked Mickey Featherstone. Did he catch your name tag? I hope you have good insurance on your grandmother, because there is no telling if she is in danger or not." That brought a laugh from everyone standing around the desk, as Delaney made his way out the door thinking about what he had just done.

As a police officer you can never really know who you are dealing with. You can't judge a book by its cover. Mickey Featherstone looked like a cop or a choir boy—but he was a cold-blooded killer who was capable of taking your life in a New York minute. Imagine stopping a guy like that and thinking he's okay—but he's not. Attitude is so important on the job. Being a professional and treating everyone the same will keep you out of trouble and alive to collect your pension. Delaney was a good kid, but he thought being tough meant kicking a handcuffed prisoner—the only problem was that prisoner was Mickey Featherstone.

Saying What You Mean and Meaning What You Say

Again, in dealing with the proper attitude in policing, I remember my regular partner taking off for the evening so I was assigned a brand new officer. Lichtenstein's leather was so new that I doubt he could have gotten his weapon out of his holster if the bad guy gave him three minutes to do so. I could tell almost immediately he wanted to make a name for himself and prove that he was going to be a tough detective one day. I wasn't impressed.

We were assigned one of the meanest and toughest foot posts in all of Harlem. Anyone who knew the area knew that you could lose your life in a fraction of a second. Later that evening we received a noise complaint to investigate that there was a man beating on a mailbox like a conga drum and singing at the top of his lungs. When we arrived on the scene, Lichtenstein immediately approached the muscular male and shouted at him, "Knock it off!" But the guy kept beating the mailbox as if Lichtenstein was invisible. Several of the drummer's friends began to smirk and laugh. If you could visualize Mike Tyson in his prime, that's how this guy looked. As I had already surmised, later he would tell me that he was recently released from Attica Prison where he bulked up lifting weights all day.

With one hand on my nightstick and the other ready to call for a back up, I allowed the new Wonder Boy, Lichtenstein, to handle what he had begun. Lichtenstein then came up with a brilliant ultimatum, "If you don't stop and move on, I'm going to beat your [posterior]!" The guy looked at my much smaller partner and completely ignored him. I leaned over and whispered in Lichtenstein's ear, "What are you going to do now?" Seeing he jumped from plan A to plan Z in one swoop, giving up every trump card a cop has, he had very few options—either beat the guy's rear, which wasn't a very good idea, or put his tail between his legs and walk away, and I wasn't about to let that happen. Lichtenstein stood there like a deer caught in the head-lights of an oncoming car. With this guy, it would have been more like an oncoming tractor trailer.

I walked passed Lichtenstein and up to the mailbox player and said, "Listen, man, could you stop playing just for a minute?" He did. I then said, "We received a noise complaint about you playing this here mailbox. I was wondering if you could do me a real big favor and stop and move on so the sergeant doesn't get on my case?" He smiled and said, "Yes sir, no problem" and walked away.

It's all about attitude. Most times if you just talk to people like a real person, they will respond in a nice way—even guys who just got out of Attica. Whether it is a Mickey Featherstone, an ex-con mailbox player, or some guy you stop for speeding, approach the individual and treat them like a decent human being. It took me a while to learn that it works. A smart cop can talk his way out of almost anything. When you practice having a good attitude you will actually have motorists you just gave a ticket to thanking you.

Attitude: A Critical Spirit in the Camp

Officer Bob Gramm was pretty much critical about everything—but especially the Police Department. One day while checking my mailbox in the main floor area of Police Headquarters, I bumped into Officer Gramm. He started complaining about a pending promotion exam I was responsible for putting together. He said, "Hey Doc, why even give the exam—everybody knows that the chief is going to make a broad sergeant no matter who scores the highest." Then he continued on to complain about everything he perceived as being broken, wrong, and hopeless with the department. As a division commander/police chaplain, I held a duel role of having to oversee the Support Services Division and be a spiritual counselor—so I didn't want to just straighten him out or ignore him either.

Rick Warren, author of the best-selling *Purpose-Driven Life*, says, "It is always easier to stand on the sidelines and take shots at those who are serving than it is to get involved and make a contribution." This is especially true in the police department. It is not unusual to hear comments like, "Those idiots in their ivory tower have no clue what it's like out here on the street" or "Do you think the brass really cares about us? What a joke! I'm only going to do what I have to do and that's it. Nobody upstairs will back you when push comes to shove." Of course there are times when some of these feelings are partially justified. I have personally worked with and for superior officers who were only concerned about their career advancement and personal benefits and rarely indicated a concern for their subordinates.

It is important to note that Officer Gramm remained on a continual downward spiral in his police career—often brought up on charges that would eventually cost him his badge for over one year. In an effort to try to restore him and protect his family, the chief of police allowed him to remain in the department as a civilian dispatcher, and later as a court liaison. As part of his probation requirements, he was assigned to me as the department chaplain. I am happy to say he eventually surrendered his life to God. I had the privilege of baptizing him in the Atlantic Ocean. Officer Gramm turned his life around—but not before he placed a shotgun in his mouth and seriously considered taking his own life.

Suicide was not a foreign phenomenon in his life. When he was a young boy his mother took her own life and left a note telling him that she hoped he and his father were now happy. That death and letter would haunt Officer Gramm all the days of his life until he became a Christian. Shortly after his baptism on a brisk day in Florida's Atlantic Ocean, he said he wanted me to join him as he finally decided to burn his mother's letter and put that pain to rest.

Officer Gramm eventually appeared before the Florida Department of Law Enforcement's review board who considered reinstating him as a police officer. A commander and I testified in Tampa on his behalf—then Officer Gramm himself was asked if he had any comments to make. He humbly stood and made one of the most compelling statements I have ever heard in my life. As he looked into the eyes of those who held his career by their vote, he softly shared that he was guilty as charged and held no ill feelings toward his superiors who he once fought while living a life of lies. He told the panel that he lost his badge for over one year and would respect a decision not to reinstate him.

It was the ending statement that touched almost everyone in the room. He earnestly said, "Sirs, there is something that can never be taken from me that has finally brought me wholeness and peace in my life; that being my salvation in Jesus Christ. I am not the same man I once was. The Robert Gramm mentioned in that report has long passed away and is gone forever. I assure you that in whatever capacity I work in Law Enforcement, I will do so in a way that honors my department and my promise to God. Thank you and may God bless you." The vote was unanimous to recommend that Officer Robert Gramm, 16-year veteran of the force, be reinstated as a police officer. He got his badge back and won numerous awards and recognitions for his outstanding contributions to the department he once had a critical spirit toward. Today, now retired, he owns and operates one of the most successful transportation companies in the Port St. Lucie, Florida area named, of course, God's Chariots.

The reason I share the Bobby Gramm story is to point out that there is usually something very deep going on in a person that acts out that way with such a critical spirit on a consistent basis. They are usually broken people who have been broken by life. A rebellious person who challenges authority most likely grew up in a very oppressive home with some form of abuse. It has been my experience that oftentimes, persons who enter the helping or service professions are persons with life experiences that have negatively affected them in broken ways. I am not suggesting that persons must be complete and whole before entering a profession of service to others; however, it is intrinsically important to progress on a spiritual, emotional, psychological, and physical journey with God leading toward healing and wholeness. That is what happened to Bobby Gramm. I love what the prophet Isaiah had to say in the 61st chapter that I will paraphrase: "The Lord binds up broken hearts. He is a comforter to those who mourn. He provides beauty in exchange for ashes. He brings gladness for mourning and praise in place of despair." I cannot begin to tell you how many broken police officers, and ministers for that matter, I have encountered who were working their service out of a base of extreme brokenness and even dysfunction. We cannot expect to indefinitely draw from a spiritual well without supplying that well.

The first thing Bobby Gramm had to admit was that he was broken and wounded by life. When we can come to that place of confession, God can take over and do the rest. Imagine carrying around that kind of weight and pain for all those years and not knowing what to do with it other than being bitter, angry, and complaining.

FOURTEEN

Self-control Is Not an Option

"But the fruit of the Spirit is love, joy, peace, patience, kindness, goodness, faithfulness, gentleness, and self-control." —*St. Paul in Galatians 5:22-23*

Police officers are expected to be in control of their emotions at all times. When I was an active police officer there were many occasions where everything in my emotional bank told me to cry, but I couldn't because I was a cop. Frankly, I can only think of one occasion when I allowed tears to well up in my eyes—and that was when a toddler fell 14 stories from an apartment window and landed in an alleyway. My partner, Dominick, and I had the awful task of securing the child's body until the medical examiner arrived. At the time both of us had small children and the thought of this happening to any parent emotionally crushed us.

Besides witnessing Dominick cry, there was only one other occasion I observed another officer openly shed tears. This is an amazing testament considering all of the pain and suffering I witnessed over the years. It was a chilly evening in Midtown Manhattan and my partner for the night was a tall, lean, and strong African American officer who, like me, was a former paratrooper. Chuck Conners was a second degree black belt in Taekwon-Do and would later go on to become a respected Police Academy instructor in martial arts. Chuck was an interesting guy who marched to a very different beat than most New York City cops. He was a student and writer of poetry, an accomplished artist in various paint mediums, and a philosopher extraordinaire. Chuck's mouth was always running—always providing philosophical perspective that was way over the heads of most cops. I enjoyed working with him. He was blatantly honest, yet he was one of

91

the most compassionate guys I've ever met. He thought that everybody who couldn't comprehend his thought process was a "knucklehead." Come to think of it, I don't ever remember Chuck using a profane word, even though profanity was part of the lingo of the NYPD.

A call barked over our radio of a reported male on fire in the entranceway of a subway station on Broadway and 42nd Street. We were just a half block away and made it to the location in under 30 seconds. Running down the steps of the subway entrance, we could smell the burning of clothing and human flesh. Making the turn down to the second landing, we discovered a Transit cop who had taken off his own coat to beat the flames rising off of a man who was screaming and rolling back and forth on the ground. This poor homeless guy had already suffered second and third degree burns over most of his body. With the help of a token booth clerk armed with a fire extinguisher and the Transit officer's coat, we were able to extinguish the fire, leaving this unrecognizable soul shivering and moaning in extreme pain.

Just moments before, while this homeless man sat on the subway floor begging for a handout, three youths drenched him in lighter fluid and set him ablaze. As the man burned, witnesses said the three youths ran up the stairs laughing at the top of their lungs. When Chuck and I got back to our car and closed the doors, he punched and cracked the dashboard of the cruiser and cried out, "How can one human being do that to another human being? Man, I just don't understand." And with that he openly cried. Honestly, I didn't know what to do at the time. All I could say was, "I know, Chuck—I know," and drove off.

Police officers are not only expected to control their emotions, but they are often challenged to control the emotions of others who are out of control. I wish I had a five dollar bill for every family dispute I found myself in the middle of, trying to calm down an irate wife or an aggressive husband or an obstinate teenager who just punched a hole in the wall. Cops are supposed to maintain their composure in every situation to help stabilize a crisis—not fuel or ignite it.

The unwritten sense that officers are always to have their emotions under control leaves anyone with a basic understanding of human psychology to ask, "Where do those emotions go?" They have to go somewhere; they don't just dissipate. Where does an officer express feelings of fear or sadness or insecurity or doubt? The officer can't share all of his or her feelings at home so as not to worry the family or surmising that the family wouldn't really understand anyway. An officer can't share everything on the job because his or her co-workers might think he or she is a "wuss." Dr. Ellen Kirschman, a leading police psychologist, says, "Officers are rewarded for maintaining emotional distance in the performance of their duty and punished for doing so in their personal relationships, where this same emotional control causes them to hurt and alienate those they love and need."[23]

It didn't take me very long in my law enforcement career to build an assorted network of emotional defense mechanisms. One form was cynical humor; making jokes about the most horrific circumstances that the average citizen would find repulsive—most of which I am even embarrassed to write about. I will, however, share one personal story of a cop-humor mechanism in action. As a police officer with the elite T.P.F. (Tactical Patrol Force) I was working another cold winter night in Harlem's 28th Precinct. Shooting cops in the "Two-eight" was almost a sport. I was assigned a foot post with my partner, Joe, a Vietnam infantry veteran who never exhibited signs of fear, thinking he was already on borrowed time. Being at West 116th Street and Eighth Avenue at ten o'clock at night is not where the common everyday working person would choose to hang out. The good and decent folks were all bedded down and locked behind their fortified apartment doors, while the night crawlers roamed the streets looking to buy dope, get high, or score some kind of deal. As Joe and I stood on the corner twirling our nightsticks, we could tell we were not liked by those who happened to cross our path.

In the routine of the night a man came running up to us and said that people were shot in an apartment around the corner. We quickly but cautiously raced down the block (It would not have been the first time that a team of cops were set up for an ambush—this time it was for real). As we entered the fourth floor apartment, we could see two bodies lying on the living room floor; one was face down and the other, still obviously breathing, was staring up at the ceiling. With guns drawn we entered the apartment and noticed that a female had been shot in the back of the head while fleeing into the bathroom, causing her to spin around and land on her face with her body halfway in the bathroom and halfway in the living room.

Since the shooters were long gone, we called for a supervisor, the detectives, and an ambulance to respond while we secured the crime scene. The female had bled out from under her face. Her blood saturated the carpet and must have soaked itself in the floor boards beneath. I slightly lifted her head only to have her brains begin to spill out, so I dropped the head where it was. Shortly thereafter a team of cops from our unit arrived to offer assistance. Our squad considered these two officers to be pretty doofy and not up to par with what an officer should be.

One of the officers asked, "Chuck, what ya got?" I said that one was dead, the big guy staring at the ceiling was still breathing, and that I wasn't sure about the female. Then my partner, Joe, said to him in an excited voice, "Hey, she's moving, Phil! Quick, turn her over!" Phil, being somewhat naïve, quickly turned her around only to find her brains spilling out from her head. I'm ashamed of what happened that night. Needless to say, I was not a Christian at the time. But both Joe and I began laughing riotously while Phil's face drained of color. He looked at us and said, "You guys are real jerks," and left the apartment to resume patrol. I would later find out that Phil wasn't "doofy," but rather a Christian who lived under a whole different set of rules.

It is that kind of sick humor that camoflauges a cop's emotions. There is this little voice in your head telling you that you can't feel anything—and if you do you can't do your job.

Many years later, in a different role as a police chaplain with a metropolitan police department in South Florida, I would encounter cop humor again. This time I was no longer that same guy who knelt down on an apartment floor in Harlem. A 65-year-old woman just had her hair done by a beautician who worked out of her house. Surmising that she was checking herself out in the rearview mirror, the woman ran a stop sign and was T-boned by a carting company truck. Although she appeared to be unhurt, the jarring of the impact killed her instantly. I arrived on the scene just as the officers were sliding her body out of the passenger door of the van, resting it on the side of the road. Once the officers were informed by another woman where the deceased was traveling from, a motor officer smirked and said to the other guys, "If she knew this was going to happen she could have saved herself some money by not having her hair done." I let it go at the time. Some of the guys laughed while others shook their heads in disbelief.

As her body was being driven off by the medical examiner, I called the motor officer aside. I looked him in the eyes and said, "Gary, I know how cop humor works, but what if that woman pulled out of the

SELF-CONTROL IS NOT AN OPTION

van was your mother? Just remember, I now have to go to her home with the sergeant and notify her unsuspecting husband that his wife of forty years will never be heard again to say, 'Honey, I'm home.'" Gary, who was usually steel cold and sarcastic, lowered his head and said, "Sorry, sir."

Shoveling Against the Tide

Over the years, if you remain in police work long enough you will run into road cops. I don't mean cops on the road, but rather R.O.A.D. (Retired On Active Duty) cops. Productivity shuts down and they just skate through each shift working toward that retirement. That is not a very pleasant way to work a career in any profession, but especially in law enforcement.

While serving as a police chaplain I was sitting in the briefing room before roll call talking to a cop who I know had turned bitter toward the job. His activity dropped and his supervisor said that the officer was basically coasting through each shift keeping a low profile. So I thought I would try to find out what was troubling this five-year veteran. He basically lamented that he was tired of locking up bad guys only to see some judge cut his prisoners loose. He said, "It's just not worth it—why put my butt on the line to have some jerk in a black robe cut the guy loose and some boss stick one up my butt for not doing something right in the process."

One time when I was standing in the Detective Bureau's office a group of school kids were being given a tour of police headquarters by a community affairs officer. One of the small kids looked up at the array of Wanted Posters on the bulletin board and inquisitively asked a detective, "Who are they?" The detective replied, "Those are people who have broken the law and who we are looking for to arrest." The little boy thought for a moment and asked a follow up question, "If you had them to take their picture, why did you let them go?"

Remember that a law enforcement officer's responsibility basically ends when you bring the criminal to justice and prepare the best case possible to secure a conviction. Other than that it is out of your control. What the judicial system decides to do is out of your control. Therefore, don't allow the appearance of a "revolving door" syndrome affect your future diligence in enforcing the law. Remain focused on what your job is and not on what it is not.

Cop Humor and Cynicism

I'd like to make one brief pause here concerning cop humor and cynicism. Cops can fall into a cynical attitude very easily if not careful. Rookies leave the police academy with high ideals and great expectations only to have some veteran officers tell them to forget about everything they were taught in the classroom. Hearing that kind of advice along with a few bad experiences with the general public and you have a strong possibility of an officer wet behind the ears, taking on the characteristics of a cynic. I have noticed that officers who are most cynical are the most insecure and unhappy. They tend to go through the motions to collect a paycheck and chip away at the 20 or 25 years needed for retirement. If you seriously think about it, that is no way to continue in a career until retirement. I know from many encounters that when persons like that retire, they will be just as miserable and cynical.

Unless cynics within the department get a handle on their problem as soon as possible, it can lead to some serious consequences. Cynical officers are often subjects of frequent civilian complaints. They are regular recipients of departmental disciplinary action. And when they are disciplined you will often hear them saying that they are being targeted or harassed by the brass—which in most cases is not true at all. Most officers don't like a steady diet of cynicism, either. And they will eventually avoid being around cynical officers for any extended period of time. I realize that some degree of professional toughness may be necessary for survival reasons, but it doesn't mean you have to be void of emotions, compassion, and sensitivity toward others.

There is a healthy balance of keeping control of your emotions during the performance of your official duties and expressing them in a healthy way that will help prevent a storage build-up of tragic experiences. Regular exposure to severe negativity will lead to emotional, relational, physical and spiritual brokenness.

Over the years I have observed unhealthy ways of coping with unexpressed emotions. Some officers, in an effort to escape from the extreme pressures of their job, resort to the regular consumption and abuse of alcohol—which is an accepted past time activity amongst many police officers. I've seen how the abuse of alcohol can be the cause of much misbehavior, poor decision making, and even dismissal from the department. In many ways it is one of the top professional hazards of the job. It is not uncommon to read about a police officer arrested for drunk driving, leaving the scene of an accident, participating in a barroom brawl, or soliciting the services of a prostitute while under the influence of alcohol.

Although not as prevalent, other officers secretly indulge in the use of non-prescribed medications, marijuana, cocaine, and other narcotics while living in constant fear of discovery from a surprise drug test. But the pain inside outweighs their willingness to stop. Though drug use may be at one end of the spectrum and cop humor and/or cynicism on the other—the one mechanism that is most prevalent and damaging to self, family and the department is isolation. Pulling back from relationships that require intimacy, these individuals will often engage in an obsession with pornography, ongoing chat room participation, lone drinking, and affairs requiring no commitment. Careful attention must be given with persons who find themselves in this condition, because it will most definitely lead to a deepened state of depression and occasionally suicide, a topic I will discuss along with Post Traumatic Stress Disorder in another chapter.

Just a word of caution to family and friends of officers struggling with an addiction problem—when you suspect a problem or you are made aware of such a problem, you have an obligation to intervene and try to get that officer the help he or she needs. It cannot be ignored because it will only get worse, have an increased negative impact on the family life, and possibly lead to an on or off duty tragedy. If you are not sure what to do, seek out the department chaplain. Police department chaplains keep all information you provide in strict confidence. I cannot tell you how many times an officer or spouse of an officer will alert me of something that I can address without the officer in question ever suspecting that I was alerted. Chaplains are an under-utilized resource that can make a healthy difference in the life of a police agency—use them.

FIFTEEN

Dealing with Anger Before It Deals with You

There is nothing worse than a cop who lives with bitterness and anger. So much of my counseling, when you get down to the core of it, deals with unresolved conflict and anger. Henry Brandt, a world renowned Christian counselor, suggests that anger is involved in 80-90 percent of all counseling. A study indicated that 80 percent of couples who verbally abuse each other ended up in some kind of physical combative contact. Recently, an officer told me in all serious-ness, "The only reason I didn't knock my wife out was that I knew I would lose my job."

Anger in and of itself is not always bad; in fact, it is part of our God-given emotional composition. However, God is not responsible for how we choose to deal with our anger. I have become angry toward injustices—and that makes sense. But we still have to be cautious on how we process, and act out the anger we feel. Conversely, I know a lot of cops who repress and internalize their anger, which leads to other problems and complications.

Let me just make a few observations. First, all humanity is sinful. When triggered and left uncontrolled, we as humans are capable of doing almost anything. Second, studies have revealed that there is a certain DNA in each of us which may or may not lend itself to an angry disposition. Lastly, so much of the way we deal with things, especially when anger is involved, can be traced back to the family models we had growing up.

A police officer's wife called to inform me that her husband punched two holes through a sheetrock wall in their living room and she didn't know how to deal with his angry outbursts. When I met

99

with the officer he told me that is how his father used to behave when he was a child.

The Bible says, "Do not make friends with a hot-tempered man, do not associate with one easily angered, or you may learn his ways and get yourself ensnared" (Proverbs 22:24-25). Another officer who had by-pass surgery informed me that he has been angry most of his life and rather than dealing with it, he repressed it. That repressed anger and bitterness had an adverse affect on his health. A female officer who was extremely angry and unforgiving of her cheating husband dealt with her anger by overeating. She put on several unhealthy pounds because of it.

When you are angry and unforgiving of another, you become a prisoner to that person and the emotions that go with it. When you allow anger, bitterness, and unforgivenss to take control of your thoughts, stress hormones are produced which cause fatigue and rob you of your joy and peace. Proverbs 15:17 says, "Better a meal of vegetables where there is love than a fattened calf with hatred." When you allow events in your past and people who have hurt you to take control of your life, you take that to bed with you and it greets you in the morning. Holding on to those feelings will just eat away at you.

Repressed anger has been clinically connected to hypertension, stroke, migraine headaches, ulcers, constipation, diarrhea, ulcerative colitis, asthma, heart attacks, grinding of teeth, and has certainly been the underlying cause of accidents while driving or working. I remember when the multi-million dollar starting pitcher for the New York Yankees, Kevin Brown, couldn't control his anger and punched a wall, breaking his hand. I guarantee you that there was more behind that than giving up a run. If you don't deal with your anger, your anger will certainly deal with you. There is no easy solution in dealing with the problem of anger. It is a complex emotion, but with willingness and God's help, it can be controlled, dealt with, and healed.

St. Paul said, "In your anger do not sin" (Ephesians 4:26). It sounds as if we are being set up by the apostle Paul; how can you be angry and not sin? Well I like the way the New English Bible translation makes this verse a little clearer and provides us with a very up-to-date understanding, not only of the nature of anger, but also of a solution: "If you are angry, do not let anger lead you into sin, do not let sunset find you still nursing it." So it is not so much the anger (the feeling) that is a problem, but rather the potential behavior or reaction that leads us into sin. If you feel angry, don't deny it. Admit it, tell someone you are angry, and begin to talk about it in a healthy way.

The Bible says not to let the sun go down on our anger. This is not only an interesting position, but one that can literally save your life. If we deal with our anger today, we forbid to allow those negative associations that come with anger to cultivate.

Here are a few Bible passages that provide great counsel regarding this whole topic of anger:

- "Refrain from anger and turn from wrath; do not fret—it leads only to evil" (Psalm 37:8).
- "Do not be quickly provoked in your spirit, for anger resides in the lap of fools" (Ecclesiastes 7:9).
- "Better a dry crust with peace and quiet than a house full of feasting, with strife" (Proverbs 17:1).
- "Better to live in a desert than with a quarrelsome and ill-tempered wife" (Proverbs 21:19).
- "A hot-tempered man stirs up dissension, but a patient man calms a quarrel" (Proverbs 15:18).
- "Like a city whose walls are broken down is a man who lacks self-control" (Proverbs 25:28).

St. James wisely informs us, "My dear brothers, take note of this: Everyone should be quick to listen, slow to speak, and slow to become angry, for a man's anger does not bring about the righteous life that God desires" (James 1:19-21). Yes, there are times when we can say that our anger is righteous anger. An officer reminded me once that Jesus became angry in the temple (Matthew 21:13). But he was angry over what the people had done in his Father's house, the temple. Jesus became angry over an injustice against God and others, but when it came to the injustice inflicted upon himself, as he hung from the cross as an innocent man, he said, "Forgive them for they know not what they do" (Luke 23:34).

St. Paul continues, "Get rid of all bitterness, rage, and anger, brawling and slander, along with every form of malice. Be kind and compassionate to one another, forgiving each other, just as in Christ God forgave you" (31-32). Friend, if you allow the sun to go down on your anger, figuratively or not, you have allowed it to go too long and it will develop into something that is ugly: resentment, bitterness, hatred, division, disunity, and sickness. Emotional, physical, and spiritual health oftentimes hinges on how you deal with your anger.

I once struggled with unforgiveness toward a key person in my life that went on for years—even after I had become a Christian. God revealed to me that I had to forgive that person. I kept negotiating with God. You know how that works? But the more I read the Bible, the more I prayed, the more I sought good Christian counsel, I eventually was able to let it go and I was set free.

Forgiveness goes against our human nature. You hit me, I hit you back. You hurt me, I hurt you, right? It all has to do with pride and stubbornness and yes, sin. The hecklers at the cross didn't ask Jesus for his forgiveness—but he initiated it and forgave them.

David Augsburger in his book, *The Freedom to Forgive*, writes: "The man who forgives pays a tremendous price—the price of the evil he forgives!"

He continues, "Forgiveness seems too easy. There should be blood for blood. Eye for eye. Yes, you can knock out a tooth for a tooth in retaliation, but what repayment can you demand from the man who has broken into your home or betrayed your daughter or ruined your reputation? So few sins can be paid for, and so very seldom does the victim possess the power or the advantage to demand payment. In most cases, 'making things right' is beyond possibility! Repayment is impossible! So here is where revenge comes in. If you cannot get equal payment or restitution out of the man who's wronged you, at least you can get revenge. Pay him back in kind, tit for tat. Serve him the same sauce. Get even with him—if you insist. But remember, to get even you make yourself even with your enemy. You bring yourself down to his level, and below. There is a saying that goes: 'Doing an injury puts you below your enemy; avenging an injury makes you but even with him; forgiving it sets you above him!'"[24]

You see, forgiveness is not a feeling, because if we left it up to our feelings we would never forgive—we would remain angry and bitter and want our pound of flesh. Listen, I am not suggesting that forgiving persons for what they did wrong to you removes the pain they caused you or somehow justifies and erases their behavior—they will have to deal with God concerning that. It is just that forgiveness does not allow the past to erase you. Deal with your anger before it deals with you.

One time I was sitting in a command briefing and I noticed that the detective commander was absolutely livid over the P.I.O. (Public Information Officer) distributing information to the press, which the commander felt was detrimental to the case of bringing a "shooter" of two innocent persons to justice. The P.I.O. was known to pander to the press and would often cause frustration with the detective division working on cases.

If anyone concentrated long enough, they could see the steam coming out of the detective commander's ears. It was obvious that nothing being discussed at the staff meeting was registering with this furious supervisor. Noticing this I scribbled a note on the back of a training document which read: "Thomas Jefferson once said, 'Whenever you get angry, count to ten.' Mark Twain said, 'When you're angry count to ten and if that doesn't work—swear!'" I slid the note over to the commander and once he read it he immediately burst out laughing and quietly lipped to me, "Thank you." And the tension was lifted. As an officer, part of your job is to defuse and not exacerbate a situation. We are to be a healing salve for wounds rather than salt.

SIXTEEN

Post Traumatic Stress Disorder

Whether it was watching the collapse of the twin towers on national television or the report of yet one more roadside bombing in Baghdad, our society has become somewhat conditioned to receiving bad news on a fairly regular basis. The one caveat, however, is that the average citizen can put down the newspaper, turn off the radio, or change the channel to something less upsetting. But exposure to violence and various forms of societal depravation is an inescapable way of life for police officers. They are called to walk into a house where a brutal and bloody homicide occurred. They discover the twisted bodies of a young family trapped in the wreckage of their utility vehicle. Human tragedy, which often becomes part of a police officer's daily life, holds with it the sights, sounds, and smells that don't go away by simply taking off the uniform and changing into civilian clothes.

Living with PTSD and Not Knowing It

In all honesty I cannot enumerate all of the critical incident stress exposure I have experienced over the years I served in law enforcement. The following are a few incidents that led me to eventually realize that I had been living with Post Traumatic Stress Disorder (PSTD) and didn't even know it.

My father saw combat in both World War II and Korea. Since I was a child I knew there was something bottled up inside of him that very few people were able to detect. The two of us are able to communicate on a different level than the rest of my family. Some people consider his behavior quirky and at times unsociable. His cold sweats or shooting straight-up into a sitting position during a bad dream has been part of his life since returning home from Korea over 50 years ago. I understood why this was happening without being able to clinically define it. The reason for the communication link between us was because we were both living with Post Traumatic Stress Disorder. At the time we didn't know it, because PTSD wasn't officially designated by the American Psychiatric Association until 1980.[25] Research indicates one-third of active and retired police officers unknowingly suffer from PTSD.[26]

During World War II when troops were extracted from the front lines of combat and returned to the States, they were processed and transported on huge and slow moving troop ships. The process of returning a soldier to his old neighborhood may have taken months. Therefore, though short in duration, there was a period of transition from the front lines to the front door of the house he grew up in. Things changed with the Vietnam conflict and every war that has since followed. When combat soldiers are extracted from the field of battle, they can be back on the block within days. Just days before going home, these soldiers have grenades and mortar rounds exploding around them, automatic weapon fire cracking over their heads, and wounded buddies shouting for a medic all around them. There is absolutely no time to transition from a world filled with violence, chaos, and instability to a quiet and familiar place of relative peace and security. Although several programs are in place to try to help Iraq War veterans make the transition—it is probably not enough. For instance, officials at Ft. Drum, New York (home of the 10th Mountain Division), created a PTSD task force to educate its leaders, troops, and community on the symptoms of PTSD. Returning soldiers with the 2nd Armored Cavalry Regiment stationed at Fort Polk, Louisiana, must be screened and complete a detailed questionnaire with follow-up screening three months later. The Marine Corps requires all returning marines to attend a four-hour Warrior Transition Program seminar to discuss PTSD. The Army offers a 24-hour-a-day hotline to help soldiers deal with PTSD.[27] But each branch is realizing that most soldiers do not seek help on their own for fear of being stigmatized or somehow hurting their careers. The same is true for police officers.

Most Americans make some room in their thinking process to understand the effects that war experiences can have on our veterans. You'll hear someone say, "He hasn't been right since he came back," or "Vietnam messed him up." We now clinically call this Post Traumatic Stress Disorder (PTSD) or Post Traumatic Stress Syndrome

(PTSS). Although our American culture is only now coming into an appreciation and respect for what our war veterans experience, the average citizen makes no room for PTSD for police officers who are exposed to critical incident stress just hours before transitioning back to their homes and neighborhoods as normal husbands, wives, fathers, mothers, and next door neighbors (*Appendix B: 25 Most Stressful Law Enforcement Critical Life Events*).

In many ways I am still processing my combat experiences fought on the streets, in the tenement hallways, on the roof tops, and in the rat-infested alleys of New York City. Even as I review my police experiences I cannot think of one time that I was provided the opportunity to process my experience of an officer dying in my arms, bullets flying around me as I rushed into a dark cellar in Harlem, seeing a woman with her face blown off, a derelict man ignited like a human torch, a baby with every bone broken in her body after a fourteen story fall, seeing dismembered body parts after an explosion at LaGuardia Airport, or engaging a deranged man in hand-to-hand combat who ripped my gun from my holster and tried to shoot me with my own weapon. Over and over again I experienced the pain, the tragedy, and the results of heinous acts committed by the criminally-minded segment of society, yet never was provided with an outlet for processing such experiences. Within hours I was expected to throw my kids up in the air, kiss my wife, run around the yard with our family dog, and have normal conversations with my neighbors about baseball and politics. How normal is that?

Experts say PTSD is not a mental illness. I thank the good Lord for that because otherwise I would be in trouble. Allen Kates, a member of the American Academy of Experts in Traumatic Stress, says that PTSD "is a normal reaction to being victimized, abused, or put in a life-threatening situation with few means of escape."[28] Looking back I can clearly see myself fitting into this definition many times over.

The Rat's Nest

During my first year out of the academy I was working in Sector Eddie in the 23rd Precinct. My partner and I received a call from Central dispatch to a "possible D.O.A. inside Apartment 4A at 408 East 107th Street—see superintendent upon arrival." Waiting in front of the premises was Carlos, the proud superintendent of a well-kept tenement in El Barrio, the predominantly Hispanic community.

Unable to gain access into the apartment, my partner, a seasoned officer, told me to remain with the superintendent while he tried to access the fire escape. Once he looked through the window of the apartment, Frank was able to see an elderly woman lying face up on the floor of the short hallway leading to the kitchen. It appeared to be suspicious and a possible homicide. Frank used his flashlight to break a windowpane, unlocked the kitchen widow, and entered the apartment. Passing the body with care not to disturb a possible crime scene, he unlocked the apartment door and let me in while calling for the detectives to respond. We then moved out into the common hallway area, secured the entrance to the apartment, and waited for the detectives to arrive.

The stench of decaying flesh was so strong it remained in my nostrils for days. When the two detectives arrived, they entered the apartment. One of the detectives was an overweight, ruddy-faced gentleman who obviously enjoyed his ale at the local hangout. With a cigar clinched in his teeth, he looked at me, a new kid in the command, and yelled, "For crying out loud, kid—go and find some coffee grains and fry them on the stove to get the stink out of here!" Addressing Frank with a much kinder and gentler tone of voice, he said, "Frank, open up all the windows and let's air this place out a little."

Detectives are a pretty unique species—especially those who work in high-crime areas of major cities. They are walking encyclopedias on criminal investigations. The experiences they possess move out of the theoretic to the practical in amazing ways. This detective took one look at the open cavity of the old lady's chest that appeared as if someone hacked at her with a meat cleaver and said, "Guys, this ain't a homicide, unless you want to charge a gang of rodents. She died of natural causes and a bunch of rats ate their way into her chest cavity and formed a nest. Pretty, huh? Call the M.E.—it will have to be confirmed—but that's what we got." Flicking his ashes on the floor and moving toward the exit, he looked at me and said, "Hey kid, you look a little pale," smirked, and disappeared into the hallway. One hour later, Frank took me to a great deli to eat a pastrami sandwich.

Tunnel Vision

My partner and I were returning to headquarters after processing a collar on the upper West Side of Manhattan in the 26th Precinct, driving south along Park Avenue where the Metro North train runs that brings commuters into the city from northern New York and Connecticut. The Metro North tracks are elevated on a stone base structure with drive/walk-through tunnels beneath the overpass.

As we were traveling south to use the Midtown Tunnel, out of the corner of my eye I spotted a man crouched down in the passageway of the tunnel doing something. Considering it was 2 a.m., it was obviously suspicious. My partner and I stopped the cruiser just south of the tunnel entrance and walked back to where I spotted the man. The second the crouched man saw my shadow, he turned instinctively like an animal in the wild, a gun in his hand. By the time I leapt and grabbed him, he had fired one round, narrowly missing my face. The distance between my face and the barrel of the gun was so close I had powder burns on my cheek. With an intense ringing in my left ear, I desperately tried to grab the suspect's weapon with both hands. He squeezed off another round, but this time the weapon didn't fire as I heard the hammer strike the cylinder. Strangely there was no report from the gun. It was pointed at my head and I wasn't sure if it fired. I thought, "Am I shot? Is this what happens when a round enters your brain—you don't hear the report of the gun?" My partner and I tackled the suspect and removed the gun from his clinched grip and placed him in custody.

After bringing him back to the precinct for booking we discovered that he had just shot two men at a party during a dispute over a woman. He claimed he didn't know that we were cops and thought we were some of the men who had pursued him from the place of the shooting. That's funny because my partner and I were wearing uniforms with big shiny silver shields and seven point police hats with shiny cap devices.

The real shock was when I brought the weapon to the department lab ballistics section for testing. The ballistics technician said that the round in the chamber was a .22 long, rim fire round. This particular round discharges when the firing pin, attached to the hammer, strikes the base of the casing on the rim. With no mechanical explanation, the firing pin struck the round dead center and the weapon misfired on the second round. The technician said that even when there is a center strike, most rounds will fire anyway. The bullet that never left the barrel of the gun was pointed directly at my forehead. It would have no doubt killed me. The previous round fired and missed my face by less than an inch. The second round was dead on and didn't fire. That morning I went home and cradled my children. For the first and only time I thought about finding a new line of work. Because of our act of bravery under fire, my partner and I were presented commendations and inducted into the New York City Police Department's Honor Legion. However, no supervisor, department psychologist, or chaplain ever helped me process what had happened.

Scavengers on the Loose

It was June of 1975 when an Eastern Airlines Boeing 747 crashed and burned during an attempted landing in the midst of an electrical storm at JFK International Airport. The unit I was assigned to that day was immediately dispatched to the scene of the crash to secure the site and search for survivors.

As we arrived at the sight of the crash during busy rush hour traffic, we could clearly see that wreckage was strewn all across a marshy area east of Rockaway Boulevard. The site resembled a battlefield similar to Gettysburg. There were bodies and luggage everywhere. There were passengers still strapped in their seats while most of the victims of the crash were burned beyond recognition or torn apart like rag dolls. I remember seeing children's toys amongst the wreckage, which was the most gut-wrenching because I had a little one-year-old at home.

The one thing I remember is that as we ran toward the crash site there were young men who were running across the field carrying luggage like scavenger vultures picking the bones of a dead man in the desert. I reached for my weapon and was going to shoot one of the looters, which was a bad tactic to say the least, when Sergeant Moreno grabbed my arm and yelled, "Chuck, don't shoot!" I am thankful he did that. This was before I became serious about my faith. I felt such a disdain for those individuals who not only disrespected the dead, but stripped them of their belongings. This wasn't Rwanda or the Sudan—it was New York City. One hundred and nine people died that afternoon just inches from the runway that could have delivered them to their loved ones and destinations. Up to that point, it was the worst single plane disaster in the New York metropolitan area. The sights and smell stuck with me and the others for a long time. Yet when all was said and done, not a single person checked with us to see if we were alright. Early the next morning I drove home listening to the Bob Grant talk radio program, entered the house, ate a banana, watched some TV, and went to bed. But where did all of that exposure to such a critical incident go? Did it just dissipate or was it shoved down into the depths of all the other memories never dealt with?

Destination: LaGuardia Airport

I cannot count the number of times I have flown in and out of La Guardia Airport in Queens, New York. Shortly after leaving active duty with the Army, I worked at the Marine Air Terminal at LaGuardia. My brother, Jerry, worked for Eastern Airlines for over twenty years at LaGuardia. I know this airport like the back of my hand. What wasn't so familiar was what I witnessed on December 29, 1975.

At the time I was assigned to the elite T.P.F. (Tactical Patrol Force). Long before court rulings on various forms of discrimination, in order to be assigned to T.P.F. an officer had to be a minimum of six feet tall. As a six-footer I was one of the shortest guys in the unit. The tactical unit was assigned to work the very toughest precincts in the city to help supplement the regular precinct officers in fighting crime. With more than 200 members, T.P.F. was headquartered on the site of the old World's Fair grounds in Flushing, Queens—just a shadow's length from Shea Stadium, home of the New York Mets. This made commuting to work very convenient for guys like me who lived in Queens or on the eastern end of Long Island.

In a routine start of our shift, we stood in a four-squad formation to receive our assignments and to be inspected by our lieutenant and squad sergeants. Each squad was assigned approximately twelve officers and one sergeant. Our roll call briefing began at 6:00 p.m. and usually lasted approximately 20 minutes. By 6:25 p.m., all 40 officers, four sergeants, and one lieutenant were headed west on the Grand Central Parkway for the South Bronx in a long caravan of cruisers and 16 seat passenger vans. We no sooner passed LaGuardia Airport, which is located two minutes from our headquarters, when we heard an emergency services officer, using our Special Operations frequency, frantically call for back-up and as many ambulances as possible. Little did we know that on that cold wintry Monday night, four days after Christmas and 48 hours from the beginning of a new year, a bomb planted by terrorists exploded in the packed main terminal of one of the country's busiest airports.

Our entire caravan was able to swing off at the Marine Terminal exit just past the Main Terminal and circle back to the place of the explosion. Pulling up to the entranceway of the TWA terminal, and

111

rushing from my van in the direction of the screams and chaos, what I was about to see could not be replicated by a Hollywood special effects engineer. There were bodies lying everywhere. Dismembered body parts were scattered over a wide area. Women were screaming and crying. Men were moaning and calling for help. The head of a woman decapitated by a large piece of flying glass lay next to the outer window frame of the terminal. Water gushed from broken pipes. Electrical wire hung from the ceiling like vines dangling from a tree. There was an obvious and clear stench of gun powder in the air. It was a bomb alright—no mistaking that. There was no way of knowing where to start, what had happened, or who was going to take charge.

Judging by the most severe place of damage, it was easy to surmise that the blast originated in a set of coin-operated lockers. The lockers and luggage carousel were blown out, both of which were reduced to pieces of twisted metal. Later I traveled up to the second level of the terminal to see if anyone was hurt above the main floor. The magnitude of the blast blew a 15 by 15-foot hole clear through the eight-inch thick concrete slab ceiling of the baggage area, driving debris into the upper ceiling of the second landing.

Finally several high ranking officers and paramedics arrived to organize some semblance of order and direction. The well-known ABC reporter, John Johnson, approached me and asked if I knew what had happened—and I recall saying something like, "It's war in there. It's beyond description." As he tried to pry more information out of me, I walked away and reentered the now cordoned off area of one of the largest crime scenes in New York City up to that time.

For the rest of the night, my unit carried bodies to a makeshift morgue in one of the undamaged terminals. Today the crime scene unit would have left the bodies where they were to take photographs and measurements—but that didn't happen on that night. We were told to remove all of the bodies as quickly as possible while medical personal either took injured victims to nearby hospitals by ambulance or treated them at an emergency on-site triage center. Then we were issued plastic bags to collect body parts.

When all was said and done, a total of eleven were killed and over 75 injured, many severely. As horrific as the scene was, it was a miracle because the magnitude of the blast should have tripled the number of fatalities and injuries. Apparently a flight had just cleared out and most of the injured were employees, limo drivers, and passengers waiting for a pickup. Mostly all of those who died were killed by shrapnel and large pieces of flying glass that traveled at great speeds. It was later determined that the bomb was the equivalent of 25 sticks of dynamite and was composed of either TNT or plastic explosives.

Tired and weary after a long endless night of carnage and an unimaginable exposure to death and dying (where I actually slipped several times on pools of human blood), our unit was relieved of duty. We made the short journey back to our headquarters, changed, and drove home. Think about that for a moment. We were all exposed to such a horrific scene of violence on a mass scale and we never spoke to a superior, a psychologist, or a chaplain.

The Night Heaven Cried for Bobby

I can honestly say that one particular *critical incident* during my police career left me with an emotional scar that had a direct nega-tive impact on my life and that of the life of my family for a number of years. On a bitter cold night in February 1980, my partner and I were patrolling one of the most dangerous areas in Harlem—the 28th Precinct. It was close to midnight and our scheduled shift of 6 p.m. to 2 a.m. was quickly coming to an end when we could head to our homes in the suburbs of Long Island.

While parked on West 116th Street and 8th Avenue, a busy noctur-nal place of criminal activity, another unit rolled up along side of us. It was two officers from a Street Crime unit assigned to our division. They asked if we would be willing to assist them in arresting someone they just spotted on West 118th Street who was wanted on a felony warrant. The plan was for the other team to enter the block and pass the suspect, then double back on foot while my partner and I closed in from the opposite direction—thus trapping the fugitive. We already knew that the suspect was known to be armed and dangerous.

Bobby, a highly decorated officer who had already been wounded twice in the line of duty and won the department's Medal of Honor, made the crucial mistake of making eye contact with the suspect as he drove by. The street-wise felon instantly read the signal and immedi-ately fled into a vacant lot. Departing from the original plan, Bobby bolted from his car and pursued the man on foot. My partner and I, along with Bobby's partner, joined in the chase. As we approached the end of the building line of one of the tenements, gun shots rang out from the inner darkness of the vacant lot. We exchanged fire, but

Bobby, who had reached the corner of the building first, took several hits as he fell to the ground. There was Bobby lying mortally wounded in the midst of broken glass, discarded baby diapers, dog excrement, and an assortment of other garbage strewn about.

I had seen that glazed-over look of a dying man many times before. If there was anything I was acutely familiar with, it was death. There was no doubt in my mind that Bobby would not make it that night. My partner, however, refused to believe the reality of his condition and ripped open Bobby's jacket in a futile effort to minister life back into his body. Looking down on my partner bent over Bobby's body and the fourth officer out in the middle of the lot, I kept yelling into my portable radio, "10-13, Officer Shot!~10-13, Officer Shot!" When the dispatcher requested our location, my mind went completely blank. "My God," I thought, "Where the hell am I?" I had no idea where we were. I thought to myself, "Take a deep breath—you're in the two-eight. You're in the 28th Precinct...8th Avenue... 8th Avenue and what? I was in a vacant lot on West 120th Street and 8th Avenue!" I could hear screaming sirens from police cars running up and down the avenues searching for us. It was a surreal experience. It felt like I was dreaming and would wake up at any minute. My partner was screaming for help. Bobby's partner, in shock, was standing in the middle of the lot, shaking and crying. What the hell was going on? Could this really be happening?

I remember turning the corner of the building and crouching down while holding my flashlight high and away from my body, trying to get a glimpse into the darkness of the backyard. I kept thinking, "Adjust your night vision. Don't walk in. Just wait." I kept moving my gun from left to right like a turret on a Sherman tank in an attempt to recognize a human target. I knew the suspect had to be hit. Moments earlier I had reached down and picked up Bobby's Smith & Wesson .38 caliber, five-shot Chief revolver and now took a moment to break open the cylinder. He had discharged all five rounds at the perpetrator. I knew this guy must have been hit. Bobby was right on top of the guy. In retrospect, I am not very proud of what went through my mind at that moment. A thought raced through my mind as I searched that backyard—that if I had discovered a wounded animal, I might have put him out of his misery. Thankfully, God protected me from committing such an unjustifiable act. The shooter, though critically wounded, managed to make it to the street, hailed a gypsy cab, and fled to a

Westchester County Hospital emergency room in Mount Vernon, telling the ER staff that he was a victim of street brawl in the Bronx.

Images flashed through my head of Bobby's lovely young wife and three children who were fast asleep. They had no clue that their husband and father would not be returning home, but rather would be receiving an inspector's funeral in a couple of days. I saw her dressed in black with Bobby's uniform hat clutched in her hand. It was strange that I would think about that as I looked at Bobby's lifeless body. Cops from all over the country would converge on a small church to pay homage to a fallen hero. Bagpipes playing "Going Home" and "Amazing Grace," a bugler playing "Taps," the 21-gun salute...I had witnessed more inspector funerals than I would like to admit.

It all happened that quickly. One minute we were developing a plan to bring down a bad guy—some small-time punk who worked the dark side of life—and the next minute, the guy you just joked with so nonchalantly is dead. The lives of three cops who were spared for whatever reason would be changed forever—not to mention Bobby's young family.

What happens after experiencing such a horrific trauma? Well, I can tell you what happened to me. I was ordered, along with the other two officers on the scene, to the 28th detective squad for debriefing. Having just been informed that the ER medical team at Harlem Hospital cut open Bobby's chest in an attempt to massage his heart and lost him, I walked into the second floor detective unit office. There we stood in the squad room filled with dozens of detectives from Major Case, Homicide, the Commissioner's Office, and Lord only knows who else.

Phones were ringing, a pin-up board was set up tracking the progress of the investigation and a uniformed officer blew past us with some forty cups of coffee. The three of us who just witnessed our coworker die stood by, emotionally drained, disoriented, and in shock. No one, including us, recognized the symptoms PTSD. It was just part of being a cop.

A detective with his nose out of joint (either sculptured in a boxing ring or in a number of Blarney Stone Bar fights) looked up in our direction and asked, "Who are yous guys?" I replied that we were the officers who were at the scene of the shooting. He turned to the center of the room and yelled, "Hey boss, these are the cops who were with the officer who was shot!" Interestingly, no one asked if we were okay.

Hey, you're a cop—suck it up and be a man, right? NYPD cops can handle anything. I said to the plainclothes supervisor, "Do you want Bobby's gun?" His eyes widened as he gasped, "Holy sh*t—you've got the cop's gun?" Then he shouted, "We've got the cop's gun!" In a state of shock I had completely forgotten that I had stuck Bobby's gun in my waistband. The boss yelled, "Jimmy, all five rounds were fired—the guy may be hit—put that out right away—we might have a wounded perp! I want all the hospitals in a one hundred mile radius checked." I could have sworn that I told someone at the scene that I had the weapon, but then again, I may have just said it to myself.

After some brief questioning and an inspection of our weapons we were taken back to the scene of the crime to walk the homicide cops through everything we experienced. As we described the positioning of Bobby's body, one of the detectives directed a beam of his flashlight onto the brick wall of the building. Just like inscriptions found on a piece of pottery during an archaeological dig, the wall told the story of how Bobby died. There were several ricochet marks on the wall, denoting the position of the suspect at the time of the first encounter with Bobby. Once the perpetrator made the turn at the corner of the building he abruptly stopped, placed his back flush against the wall, and extended his shooting arm with his weapon ready for the first officer to reach the kill zone. Once Bobby made the corner, the bad guy opened fire. Mortally wounded with a pierced heart, a bullet wound through his wrist, and one other wound in his shoulder, Bobby courageously returned fire, desperately firing in the direction of his opponent's muzzle flash. I believe it was Bobby's bullet that wounded the suspect, though we'll never know because he refused to allow the surgeons to remove it from his body. Convicted of killing a cop, he was sentenced to life in prison without a chance of parole and still carries a piece of lead from that dark cold night in the two-eight.

Again I ask, what happens after experiencing such a horrific trauma? Nothing out of the ordinary. I drove home to Long Island at eleven the next morning. My wife asked me how everything went at work. I answered, "Everything went fine, honey. Everything went just fine."

SEVENTEEN

Battling Stress

Experts contend and life experience prove that Post Traumatic Stress Disorder has a variety of ways of acting out. Some common symptoms can be hypervigilance, being jumpy around sudden sounds, mild depression and anxiety, and trouble sleeping at night, or having nightmares. In most cases severe symptoms will diminish over a period of time; however, some intense symptoms may not leave so easily. An officer may feel consistently restless, unable to concentrate on one thing for long periods of time, or become easily disturbed, agitated, and angry. Oftentimes spouses cannot understand why their husband or wife is acting so strange—why he or she is not communicating. Deep down in the recesses of an officer's memory are the images of a traumatic stress incident. That causes a subconscious effect on an officer's relationships and overall well-being. The morning after the incident, the city resumes business as usual and for the most part, the officer is expected to do the same. The very next night after Bobby's death, I was working in the South Bronx just as if nothing happened.

A simple way to explain what happens when someone is exposed to sudden trauma or stress is that the body responds by releasing adrenaline. When suddenly increased levels of adrenaline is released it also increases a person's heart rate, raises their blood pressure, and etches into the mind vivid memories.

According to Dr. Roger Pitman, a psychiatry professor at Harvard Medical School, quoted in *Newsweek*, "The rush of adrenaline creates memories that intrude on everyday life and, without treatment, can actually hinder survival." I neither have the expertise nor any evidence that would suggest that every single police officer responds to sudden trauma or acute stress in the same way. However, through personal experience and in working with many police officers, I believe that

117

some preliminary follow-up care should be offered to any police officer who has been exposed to such conditions. The healing process begins with intervention. The mere fact that the officers can feel as if their department cares about their wellbeing is a stabilizing plus in any agency.

Victims of trauma should be encouraged not to stuff their emotions, which most cops do as a coping mechanism. Why do you think many departments have a heart bill benefit? Ignored damage to the mental and emotional wellbeing of a police officer can have secondary effects on the officer like heart disease, cancer, strokes, migraine headaches, and various relational disorders.

It would be good to add just as a note of observation that I have met many police officers who were conditioned to stuff their emotions long before they entered the police force. Some were combat veterans who were hardened by their exposure to violence and death in war. Others experienced violence and having their emotions stifled by an aggressive or abusive parent growing up. I would say that out of the last ten police officers I have counseled for marital or disciplinary problems, nine of them grew up in dysfunctional and abusive homes where the expression of feelings was discouraged.

Prayer As an Answer to Stress

As if we need to be reminded, interpersonal relationships create a big stress factor. In other words, people can stress you out. It might be the people you serve, your supervisors or subordinates, your in-laws or out-laws. Good people skills are absolutely necessary to be a police officer. Oftentimes we can reduce the stress experienced through relationships by working on ourselves rather than trying to work on others. We need to work on changing our own attitudes, prejudices, and predispositions rather than being bent on changing others.

Jesus once warned, "Why do you look at the speck of sawdust in your brother's eye and pay no attention to the plank in your own eye? How can you say to your brother, 'Let me take the speck out of your eye,' when all the time there is a plank in your own eye? You hypocrite, first take the plank out of your own eye, and then you will see clearly to remove the speck from your brother's eye" (Matthew 7:3-5). We need to always take a serious look at ourselves first.

A good way to do this is to sit down and begin to inventory all those things, people, and circumstances in your life that are producing stress. Then number them beginning with the most stressful. Once you have identified these areas of stress and have prioritized them, determine what measures are in your control to alleviate or eliminate them. It is like the old saying that was shared with me by a dear Nigerian friend of mine who once asked me, "Brother Chuck, how do you eat an elephant?" When I responded that I thought the exercise was foolish, he replied, "You eat an elephant one piece at a time."

When you look at the totality of all these stress points in your life, it may appear to be overwhelming and as big as an elephant that cannot be consumed or eliminated. But if you eat away at this enormous stress hypoderm in your life one piece at a time, slowly but surely you will begin to reduce the enormity of it all. The stress points low on your list can be dealt with in short order. The more difficult ones can be dealt with over time and with some help. If you discover that certain points will remain fairly consistent, consider ways in which you can strengthen yourself to better cope with them.

Of course, ultimate peace comes from God. St. Paul said, "Do not be anxious about anything, but in everything, by prayer and petition, with thanksgiving, present your requests to God. And the peace of God, which transcends all understanding, will guard your hearts and your minds in Christ Jesus" (Philippians 4:6-7).

Let me break out some of these areas so as to be more effective in your effort to lead a less stressful life beginning with prayer. The more time you spend in prayer each day, the more strength you will have to cope with stressful moments and circumstances. I begin each day with a short prayer before I even get out of bed. I pray, "Lord, help me to be out of control today, so that you may be in full control of my life." When you begin your day with that kind of prayer you will begin to receive wisdom, discernment, peace, and strength throughout the day.

Maybe it would work best for you in the early hours of the morning before the rest of the family begins to stir. Maybe it would work best late at night after arriving home from a 4 p.m. to midnight shift. I know some officers who find that quiet time during their lunch break sitting in their squad car. Wherever and whenever you choose to have your prayer and meditation time, make sure you have this time as part of your daily routine.

Not long ago, a police officer informed me that he didn't know how to pray. He discovered that he didn't know what to say and felt very awkward sitting and trying to formulate anything that resembled a prayer. There is really no set way to pray; however, I once heard someone speak about using the acronym A.C.T.S. to structure a prayer.

A=Adoration: Many people go into prayer like the cracking sound of a M-60 machine gun. "Lord, help me, give me, lead me, provide me...me, me, me." The Bible says that God inhabits the praises of his people. Adoration means that you come into God's presence and begin to worship and adore him. Remind God of how much you love him and how much you revere him. This will bring you into a heightened spiritual state of receiving.

C=Confession: Begin to make things right with God through personal confession. The psalmist writes, "Search me O God and know my heart: see if there is any offensive way in me" (Psalm 139:23,24). Make this a daily confession.

T=Thanksgiving: After confessing, thank God for all the things he has done for you.

S=Supplication: Ask God to direct and empower your life. Pray for others, world issues, the President, your church leaders, and for your relationships with friends and family. Pray for your chief, other supervisors, fellow officers, and civilian workers in the department. And when you have exhausted yourself of praying for others, then begin praying for your personal needs.

There are many ways to pray, but this is one that has helped me to structure my prayer life. Thousands of years ago, King David shouted, "This is the day the Lord has made; I will rejoice and be glad in it" (Psalm 118:24). He goes on to say in that very same chapter that we are to give thanks to God because he is good and that his love endures forever. It's not a bad way to start your day.

EIGHTEEN

Police Suicide

There is an alarming truth that most law enforcement administrators are either unaware of or are too caught up in the busyness of their duties to address; that is the fact that suicide by police officers is on the rise. More law enforcement officers take their own lives than are killed by armed attackers or duty-related accidents. In fact the number of deaths due to suicide is two to three times the number of line of duty deaths among law enforcement agencies and emergency workers.[29] According to the National Association of Chiefs of Police, every year more than 300 police officers commit suicide—that is 30 percent greater than the general population in the United States. In the NYPD alone, between January 1995 and April 1997, the number of suicides was 78.[30]

When a police officer takes his or her own life, members of that agency are emotionally impacted in devastating and debilitating ways. This is simply because police departments operate like a family unit. Although there may be griping, disunity, and dysfunction at times—like any other normal family—members are still willing to lay down their lives for each other. This is something very different from most professions. It is why the suicide of a fellow officer is listed as one of the top eight critical incidents within the emergency services community.[31] Dr. Ralph Slovenko, a law professor at Wayne State University Law School, states, "Police suicides can devastate the morale of entire agencies and leave individual officers with intense feelings of guilt, remorse, and disillusionment; many feel they should have done something to prevent the suicide."[32] I do not wish to imply that officers should walk around with feelings of guilt that they could have prevented an individual from taking his or her own life. However, I would like to suggest that there is a very strong likelihood of preventing many suicides through practicing good observation and listening skills and taking the initial steps of intervention. During a seminar I attended on police suicide, the instructor said that every suicide has a history. Patterns and signals occur and can be identified.

Post Traumatic Stress Disorder and other high levels of related stress factors are big contributing reasons for such elevated numbers of suicide in police work. There are a number of causes that can lead an officer to consider taking his or her own life. Sergeant Michael Tighe of the New York City Police Department once said, "Suicide among police officers is a dramatic example of what happens when those who are entrusted with the protection and care of others fail to protect and care for themselves." And that is so true.

A survey of 500 law enforcement officers conducted by the National P.O.L.I.C.E. Suicide Foundation, Inc. discovered that 98 percent of those surveyed said they would consider suicide under one or more of the following circumstances:[33]

• Death of a child or spouse
• Loss of a child or spouse through divorce
• Terminal illness
• Responsibility for co-worker's death
• Killed someone out of anger
• Indictment
• Feeling alone
• Sexual accusations
• Loss of job because of conviction of a crime
• Being locked up

As can be clearly seen in all of the above reasons, there is a sense of a loss of control over one's life. Cops are always called to the scene of trouble to help resolve problems. They are to be emotionally detached and calm, cool and collected. That often translates into their personal off-duty lives as well. To show pain or emotional unsteadiness is unacceptable in the minds of most officers. Along with the cop persona that has developed over the years, most cops think that expressing emotional breakdown is a sign of weakness of not being able to cut it. And yes, even becomes the brunt of many locker room jokes. This is one of the main reasons officers will not seek help to try to navigate out of their valley of depression on their own.

Experiencing repressed feelings, marriage problems, financial problems or possibly being under investigation—causes the individuals to feel a sense of desperation—a sense that there is no way out of their situation. One expert states that about 90 percent of the time, officers were drinking when they shot themselves. Alcohol is a depressant and if you are already depressed, the condition only worsens if you consume alcohol. Statistics indicate that older officers tend to commit suicide due to physical illness, alcoholism, or impending retirement where there is a sense of losing their identity.

Fellow officers, but especially supervisors and administrators, should be on the lookout for signs of an officer in trouble. (See Appendix C: Recognizing Problems Checklist.) I have seen far too many times where a police agency waits until an officer takes his or her own life before they admit that there may have been earlier signs of a problem. The time to act is early, not after the fact. The following are some signals officers and supervisors should be paying attention to:

Common Police Suicide Warning Signs:

- An officer who starts having a high number of off-duty accidents.
- A rise in citizen complaints about aggressiveness.
- A change in personality in which a sullen officer suddenly becomes talkative or an officer who is normally very vocal becomes silent and withdrawn.
- The officer starts giving away prized possessions or telling friends they will be missed.
- The officer suddenly writes a will.
- A sudden interest or disinterest in religion.

It's the job of all officers, supervisors, and administrators to look out for the wellbeing of their contemporaries and subordinates. What could be more threatening or drastic than a co-worker considering suicide? Taking this a step further, the responsibility becomes even greater for a Christian police officer, supervisor, or administrator. Why? Well, the Apostle Paul tells us in Romans 13:8 that we fulfill all the commandments by loving our neighbor as we love ourselves. Just as we wish no harm to come to us or those whom we love the most, we should be equally as concerned about everyone—but especially a fellow police officer. We are our brother's keeper.

When I was an active law enforcement officer I discovered one of the greatest positions of influence over most individuals was that of a patrol sergeant. Just as the non-commissioned officer is the backbone of the military, so too are the front-line supervisors in a police department. Good and attentive supervisors not only concern themselves with crime patterns and making sure assignments are completed in a timely fashion, but effective supervisors also get to know those who work for them. By knowing personality traits and the way their officers think and work, front-line supervisors are in the best position to monitor subordinates for signs of depression and other abnormal behavior patterns. Just as sergeants inspect the troops for proper uniform and equipment—spot checks should be made on a regular basis as to the emotional wellness of their subordinates.

There are a few tips that fellow officers and supervisors can arm themselves with in dealing with a suicidal cop. First, don't hesitate to speak openly about suicide. You can't put the idea in anyone's head if it isn't already there. Ask directly, "Are you thinking of killing yourself, committing suicide, taking your own life?" When I am counseling a depressed officer as a chaplain, I do not hesitate to ask that officer that very question. Second, be assertive. Communicate your understanding and ask what is causing such pain. Clearly say that the pain can be managed and that there are other ways to solve these problems. Let the person know that getting help is a sign of strength, not weakness, and that it takes guts to face your problems and yourself. Always offer hope—do not commiserate with the individual. Third, be honest in describing your own experiences with depression, hopelessness, or, if applicable, thoughts of suicide that at one time or the other may have crossed your own mind. Talk about what specifically helped you get through troubled times. Fourth, stick with the officer. Get involved by suggesting that there is help available. Ask the troubled officer for permission to call the chaplain, pastor, or psychologist and go with the officer to the appointment. Reassure the officer that you will help get him or her through—that you will be there.[34]

Dr. Paul Quinnett, in an article that appeared in the FBI Law Enforcement Bulletin, introduces a new, direct suicide intervention methodology called QPR, which consists of three bold steps that were somewhat covered in my previous paragraph. (1) *Questioning* the meaning of possible suicidal communications, (2) *Persuading* the person in crisis to accept help, and (3) *Referring* the person to the appropriate resource.[35] Dr. Quinnett contends, and I would agree, a timely and caring confrontation about a hinted plan of suicide, together with an immediate referral or plan of action is critical. When a supervisor or fellow officer intervenes it brings a sense of control and hope into a situation that is out of control and appears to be hopeless. It is important to remember that if treated aggressively, 70 percent of depressed, suicidal people will respond favorably in a matter of a few weeks.[36] The good faith effort to prevent the suicide of a fellow officer is not a matter of choice, but a matter of duty. Always remember, early intervention could save your buddy's life.

Something May Be Wrong, but Is It My Business?

"My dear friends, if you know people who have wandered off from God's truth, don't write them off. Go after them. Get them back and you will have rescued precious lives from destruction and prevented an epidemic of wandering away from God" (James 5:19-20, The Message).

The call came into my office at about 3:30 p.m. that one of the deputies from the County Sheriff's Office shot himself. Although I worked as a chaplain for the municipal police department, I had a great relationship with the S.O. and especially their chaplain. Within ten minutes I was in the emergency room, working my way through a crowd of officers standing by ready to donate blood if necessary. I no sooner entered through the doors of the emergency room than I discovered the officer sitting up in a daze with a swollen face and bleeding from his mouth and nose into a metal pan held beneath his chin. Obviously he was shot, but where was the entrance wound? I soon found out from one of the nurses that he had placed his duty weapon up to the pallet of his mouth and pulled the trigger hoping it would travel to his brain and kill him. But miraculously, the bullet smashed through his pallet, traveled up through his nasal cavity and lodged there, stopping short of entering his brain.

In a matter of minutes, an emergency room surgeon entered the area where the officer sat on a gurney protected from public view by pull curtains and said: "Officer, I've got good news—you're going to make it." With that, the officer punched the top surface of the padded gurney and had to be restrained. It was news he wasn't hoping for. He was hoping that the news would be that he would die.

This officer apparently got himself mixed up in an extramarital affair and was preparing to leave his wife for the other woman. Earlier that day he drove up to tell his daughter, who was a first year student at the university. Apparently she became very upset and told him that she disowned him as a father. The news hit him pretty bad. He had two hours to think about what was going on in his life as he drove back home. He wasn't sure if he still loved his wife. He wasn't certain whether this other woman was someone who he really wanted to be with—and now his daughter had walked away from him. For weeks, if not months, he lost weight, and started drinking more than usual. Other officers who worked with him knew that he was in a bad way and knew of some of what he was dealing with. Basically all of them said the same thing: "I knew he was having problems at home and seeing this other woman. I knew he was going in a bad direction but it was personal and I just wanted to mind my own business."

Fortunately, this particular officer lived. He went on to undergo numerous reconstructive surgeries in Miami that were offered pro bono by doctors who liked cops. He lost his job and later he lost both his wife and his girlfriend. I am not sure what ever happened with his daughter. He had to live with a speech impediment and the last thing I heard was that he was living with his parents in a deep state of depression as a high candidate to attempt taking his life again.

Could this have been prevented? No one can really answer that question with absolute certainty. But what if one of his supervisors or fellow officers had stepped in and offered to take him out for lunch or sat him down and counseled him? What might have happened if a good Christian buddy invited him home for a meal with his family and retired to the TV room just to be his friend and say that he was there for him, to have a word of prayer with him, or to invite him to attend church? I believe there would have been a strong probability that this officer would have sought help and would have been prevented from squeezing that trigger on his Sig-Sauer 9mm service weapon. We are our brother's keeper. Minding our own business when someone is in a deep state of depression is never the right thing to do. (See Appendix B for the Suicide Intervention Checklist for Peers.)

Suicide crosses the minds of many people from time to time, but is either a fleeting thought they get control over or they can't think of a quick and relatively painless way to accomplish it. However, a police officer has a firearm available at all times; and so it is easier to act impulsively—especially if he or she is under the influence of alcohol. This is proven by the fact that 95 percent of all police suicides are committed with a firearm.[37] That availability of a firearm can instantly bring tragedy.

When I was a narcotics detective in the Organized Crime Control Bureau's Narcotic's Division, I worked with a Hispanic undercover officer who was always upbeat and was known to have a good family life, or so we thought. One day when I reported to work, I was informed that in the fit of anger while drinking and arguing with his wife, he pulled out his weapon, placed it to his head, and pulled the trigger, blowing out his brains right before his startled wife. What made him do that? Perhaps his inner rage that was never dealt with was at fault. Certainly his excessive drinking that night played a major role. Was he suffering from PTSD, because he had previously been in a shootout? We'll never really know. But that firearm and alcohol were ever present, just like so many times before.

There is a hush of silence amongst the rank and file when it comes to the topic of suicide and policing. Whatever you do, you make sure that it is not swept under the rug. Be a catalyst in making certain that your department is talking about it; that there is sensitivity training offered on the subject and that the administration is on board. Engender a work environment where officers who are struggling with depression do not have to fear that they will lose their job, harm their careers, or be labeled in any way should they come forward and ask for help. Departments that encourage their officers to seek help and display a willingness to assist them in getting well will have a better chance of reaching troubled and desperate officers than departments that have strict policies that only cause a troubled officer to hide the problem. An individual must be reminded that depression is treatable and that every problem in life is solvable over time.

Some behavioral experts say that supervisors should also keep an eye out for officers who all of a sudden become recklessly heroic on the job. There are reported cases where officers who were once very cautious in their street tactics begin to take unnecessary risks so that if they do get killed in the line of duty, they die with honor and their family is taken care of with increased survivor benefits. Whether this theory can be proven or not, just be aware of anyone who regularly starts taking illogical risks while on patrol.

I must reiterate that it is of critical importance for the administration level of law enforcement to recognize that suicide in policing is not the next town's problem. It could be yours. Awareness and prevention begins with the office of the chief.

The following is a modified version of a poem that was written by John Rowan for Vietnam Veterans. It was modified, with permission from the author, by Cheryl Rehl-Hahn, to reflect the suicide tragedies taking place everyday among our American law enforcement community.

The Other Side of the Wall[38]

In Washington, D.C.
in Judiciary Square
there stands a blue-gray
marble wall with the names
of more than 14,000
men and women.
This is the official list of the
National Law Enforcement
Officers killed in the line of duty.
But, there is
ANOTHER SIDE OF THIS WALL
Also containing a list
with at least three times
as many numbers
—and steadily growing—
of those men and women
who were victims of
an American war.
They died away
from the streets of battle
so they are not as noticeable.
Their deaths were self inflicted,
ending years of inner torment,
and surmounting stress,
related to tragedies they
witnessed everyday.
But no matter how they died,
They were still Police Officers.
Victims of a war fought
right here in the battlefields
of American streets.
And the list will continue to grow

on the other side of the wall,
until those of us still living can
win the war on prevention with
proper education and awareness
of this tragic epidemic.

NINETEEN

Take Care of Your Body

Police shift work creates all kinds of problems for police officers and their families. The strain of trying to adjust to abnormal hours contributes to a higher degree of divorces and a greater risk of developing physical problems due to poor eating habits and insufficient sleep. The National Sleep Foundation, an independent nonprofit organization dedicated to improving public health and safety, states that the majority of people who work shift work do not get enough quality sleep. And when a person is sleep deprived, they tend to think, move, and react more slowly, make more mistakes, and have difficulty remembering things. This leads to lower job productivity and can cause an increase in accidents. A lack of quality sleep is associated with irritability, impatience, anxiety, a lack of concentration, moodiness, and depression. These symptoms can cause a real strain and become a major problem in a family relationship. Shift workers experience more stomach problems, especially heartburn and indigestion, menstrual irregularities, colds, flu and weight gain than day workers. Heart problems and higher blood pressure are more likely.

Good cooperation and teamwork is required in order for police officers and their families to remain healthy and relationally strong. This necessitates great sacrifice on the part of a spouse and children in helping create the environment that will allow the officer to acquire the maximum time of uninterrupted sleep. When I was working midnights and my wife and I had two small, energetic children in the house, I was thankful that our master bedroom was on the second floor and the opposite end of the house from where the children played and watched television. But there were other little things my wife was able to do to allow me a good, solid stretch of sleep. She would disconnect or shut off the ringer on the phone in our bedroom. That little measure can make a huge difference. If she went out shopping or took the kids to the park, she would turn the ringer off on our main phone as well and lower the volume on the answering machine so messages were received without a phone ringing or a loud speaker announcing the caller's voice. I also found having the room darkened was extremely helpful in getting to sleep and staying asleep during daylight hours. Dark drapes, special curtains, or shades can be installed that block out most sunlight fairly well. One other thing I appreciated about my wife was that she never left an unmade bed for me to crawl into. It was always made, often times with fresh sheets and pillow cases, which felt very welcoming and restful. Common sense details can make a tremendous difference.

If you are commuting a considerable distance after working an extended midnight shift, serious care and consideration should be given about whether or not to drive an automobile. There is a disparaging difference in vehicular accidents involving police officers commuting home after a midnight shift and officers who work the day shift or the 4 p.m. to midnight shift.

At approximately 4 a.m. one morning, though dog tired, I forced myself to attempt to drive home so I could sleep in my own bed after an extended 6 p.m. to 2 a.m. shift. I could not account for driving over two exits on the Long Island Expressway. I eventually fell asleep at the wheel, lost control of my car, and my vehicle crossed two lanes and entered the median. I was abruptly awakened by the sound of gravel striking the bottom of my car. I jammed on my brakes and was able to bring the car to a stop before it struck the guardrail. That was a real, close encounter with what could have been a great tragedy. Think smart and make wise decisions. If your precinct or district has an officer's dorm, lie down for a few hour's sleep before traveling home or before making a morning court appearance. If you must drive home, leave the car window open, play the radio, and occasionally stop to either take a brisk walk around the car or a 15-minute power nap.

Caring for Your Body

There are interesting extremes of physical conditioning or lack thereof witnessed throughout the law enforcement community. On one end of the spectrum are the gym warriors who work out regularly, pumping iron in order to roll up the uniform shirt sleeve a turn or two to show their bulging biceps. They drink all kinds of concoctions and high-protein shakes, juices, and potions. Or they can be long distance runners who jog dozens of miles each week to keep their cardio-vascular system working and weight off. On the other end of the spectrum are the all too familiar beer gut sporting, cigarette or cigar smoking, doughnut eating officers who take two steps into a foot chase and say, "I'll get you next time." I am not insinuating that the latter type is bad in and of itself. However, just as a cursory note, I have also witnessed officers who become so obsessed and preoccupied with their bodies, that they know very little else but their personal physical fitness and appearance. They develop a serious case of vanity. That can become a form of self-worship and can draw one's attention from other important matters and relationships.

I believe it is important to remember that in order to be an effective law enforcement officer, you do not have to look like Arnold Schwarzenegger or be as thin as Twiggie. However, a cop must be in good physical condition in order to be physically and mentally sharp and effective on the street.

You may wonder why all this talk about the body matters to a minister. Well, God is interested in the whole person when it comes to health and wholeness. I have counseled with many people who are physically unhealthy due to their holding on to unforgiveness, bitterness, and built-up anger. Then there are officers who abuse their bodies with what they ingest: junk food, alcohol, and nicotine products. They become overweight, undernourished, inactive, and unhealthy. Couple this with stress and unusual working hours and you have a prescription for disaster.

The Bible refers to our physical body as a temple or dwelling place of God's spirit. No matter what kind of relationship you have with God, you are his creation. If we begin to view our bodies as God's dwelling place, we then have a different attitude about respecting and caring for it. I often chat with officers who say they struggle with depression, chronic fatigue, sleep disorders, and shortness of breath. They tell me that the job sucks, the bosses are jerks, and their spouse is driving them up the wall. They regularly drink alcohol, consume large quantities of caffeine, ingest far too much junk food and sugar products, and wonder why they feel that lousy.

Looking back to the Garden of Eden it becomes quite clear that God never intended for us to live that way. The psalmist, David, says that our bodies are fearfully and wonderfully made (Psalm 139:14).

And indeed that is true. Our bodies are wonderfully made, but how we take care of them will determine if they will remain wonderful. Just imagine what would happen if you didn't regularly change the oil in your car's engine or if you never tuned it. Your car would not run properly and would eventually stop functioning altogether. The same is true with our bodies. We must find ways to be more vigilant in living stress-reduced lives. We need to supply our bodies with proper food and other nutrients. We need to exercise our bodies and drink plenty of water. We need to get outdoors and breathe fresh air. Finally, we need to learn how to get the proper rest our bodies require in order to function well.

Proper Exercise

Unlike most occupations where employees can pretty much predict what they will be doing during the workday, police officers never know what they will face at the beginning, in the middle, or during the final minutes of their tour. Cops can go from a lull of doing nothing to a full speed foot chase with someone ten or more years younger. Study after study has proven that cops are at a greater risk of experiencing a heart attack than most professions. One study revealed that police officers face more than twice the risk of suffering from heart disease than the general public and attributes the cause to job and lifestyle factors.[39]

Researchers have found that job related stress, rotating shifts, poor diet, and lack of exercise are key reasons police officers have a higher rate of heart attacks, strokes, hypertension, and other forms of cardiovascular disease. When you add bad habits like smoking and alcohol consumption, the numbers jump even higher.

Good aerobic exercise will not only strengthen your cardiovascular system, it will also help you release stress. Aggressive exercise like swimming, running, racketball, and brisk walking increases the body's discharge of hormones that promote positive aggression. It is always hard to put on the workout clothes and do it, but once you finish a good workout routine, you feel good about yourself and you will discover that you have much more energy. Due to work-related stress, police officers must exercise. It really isn't an option; it's a matter of survival. There are numerous books written on the subject of proper exercise and fitness and a plethora of gyms you can join that have professional trainers on staff to start you on a balanced exercise program.

It will be one of the best investments you ever made. You owe it to yourself, your family, and the people you were sworn to protect to stay in shape.

Proper Nutrition

Cops are notorious for bad eating habits. All those jokes about cops and donuts may be for a reason—though I must say that most cops I know don't like doughnuts. Police officers consume large quantities of coffee and live off of quick take-out meals high in fat content and loaded with salt. As the studies have shown that continuing to maintain an unhealthy diet, coupled with poor sleep and stress, will eventually take its toll on the body.

By maintaining a good nutritional diet you will not only increase your energy level, but you will also decrease your stress level and sharpen your mind and reflex timing. I have read numerous articles and books on good nutrition and its positive effects on a person's life and relationships. I once read somewhere that people carry between five and 20 pounds of toxic poisons and wastes inside their bodies. And if ways are not found to reduce or eliminate those poisons, the body begins to break down under the stress, we become sick, and our lives are negatively impacted.

When you eat fruit and vegetables, and drink lots of water, your body begins a cleansing process. Supplemented with high protein meats like poultry and fish will bring a change in your energy level and appearance in a very short period of time. I have listed suggested readings on proper nutrition in the Appendix at the end of the book. Take the time to eat properly, exercise, and get sufficient rest. It is a prescription for a healthy and highly productive life.

Being a Professional: Appearance Counts

Ever since I can remember, in addition to wanting to be a police officer with the NYPD, I wanted to either be a Marine or a paratrooper. In high school I would doodle on my notebooks the symbols of the U.S. Marine Corps or paratrooper wings. I knew either one of the two was the finest and most elite forces in the world and I wanted to be part of the best. I eventually would have my dream become a reality and became both a paratrooper and member of New York's finest.

During my military career I was taught early on that appearance made the first and perhaps the most significant impression when someone looks at you. I can remember traveling through a major airport terminal and seeing soldiers looking as if they were wearing a duffle bag for a uniform. Their gig-lines were off-center, pants and shirt wrinkled, hat on crooked, and shoes looking as if they were shined with a Hershey bar. I almost wanted to say, "Hey leg (a term used for non-paratroopers) get down and give me 50 pushups!" Paratroopers and Marines are a different breed. Their uniforms are always squared away and tell the world what team they play for. Their gig-lines are straight, boot toes highly polished, creases in their pants, and shirt razor sharp. Sometimes I wouldn't even sit down so as not to have my shirt rise up from being tucked into my pants. The best knew it, and wanted everyone else to know it.

Well, this practice translated into my police career. Before uniform shirts had factory-sewn pleats, I either paid a good neighborhood tailor to sew them in or I would personally wash, starch, and iron my shirts with two razor sharp pleats in the front and three in the back. I always had a lint brush or an inverted roll of masking tape in my locker to remove lint from my uniform hat, pants, chocker, and coat.

I used to have high crime "A House" cops say to me, "What for? You're working in the ghetto...let the guys working in Queens and Staten Island dress up like tin soldiers." That wasn't my philosophy. When I turned out for roll call inspection, I wanted to be absolutely squared away. It was important for me to display a military presence not only to the public, but to my colleagues and superiors as well. I knew before officers ever spoke their first word they had already gained the respect of the person they were addressing.

The overweight cop who hasn't seen his toes in years and whose uniform tie could be dipped into hot water and make a fresh pot of coffee or vegetable soup commands very little respect on the street. But when you approach someone standing tall, his or her uniform well maintained, hat bill wiped clean with a damp cloth, shoes highly polished—the public's trust level rises and the bad guys think twice before making a stupid move.

One night on the 6 p.m. to 2 a.m. shift in the South Bronx, I was working with a cop named George who was a fill-in partner for the night. George was out of shape, had unkempt hair, and wore a uniform that looked like a potato sack draped over his body. Honestly, it was embarrassing working with him. About four hours into our shift we pulled over a car that had its tail light out. The car pulled over and we asked the driver to exit the vehicle because he appeared jittery for a guy with just his taillights out. He didn't have a license or a registration and was very hesitant about answering some of the most routine questions. One thing I noticed was that he kept shifting his eyes from me and then to my partner. Sometimes I would be talking to him, but he would be looking at George. And then it happened. In a split second when I was looking at something on the car just two feet from him and my partner, he jumped George and tried to remove his service revolver from the holster. After a brief tussle, we subdued him, handcuffed him, and took him to the 44th precinct. It wouldn't be long before we discovered why he attempted his getaway. He was wanted in Florida for homicide. We also discovered why he went for George. As long as my prisoners cooperated, I always treated them with dignity and respect. This would often lead to further cooperation or even provided information to help with future investigations. This prisoner, however, said that after he sized George and I up, he knew he had a better chance with George because he gave the appearance he was the easier to take down. There was no doubt in my mind that my squared-away demeanor gave him that impression, even though George was a fifth degree black belt.

————————————■TWENTY■————————————

Leadership and Supervision

B eing a boss is more than taking a test. The first thing that must be recognized is that leadership is a place of privilege. Having gone through the ranks myself, I realize the hard work, study, and above average performance that is needed to be elevated to a position of leadership and trust. Something I tried to practice both as a supervisor in the police department and as an officer in the army, was not only to enrich, enhance, and sharpen my own career—but also to use the wonderful opportunities to enrich the lives and careers of those who worked for me.

When I was promoted to a sergeant, I immediately realized the newfound sphere of influence I could have on others, whether negative or positive. The chevrons sewn on my uniform sleeves meant more than changing in the supervisor's locker room, driving in a newer and better radio car, or enjoying the benefit of a raise in pay. It placed me in a significant place within the structure of an organization to make a difference. Sadly, I have witnessed mid and upper management lose their connectedness with their subordinates and their passion to contribute to the well-being and advancement of their department and become mainly focused on what they can receive from the system. I once sat in a Command Staff briefing consisting primarily of commanders and above in rank that were so self-absorbed in squeezing as much as they could from the municipality they worked for that they exhibited little or no concern for the people beneath them nor the tax payers they worked for. I take great pride that I can run into subordinates today who once worked for me and know that they would remember me as a boss who never shrugged my responsibility to care for them and the others they worked with.

As a pastor I have numerous titles: minister, reverend, elder, and shepherd. I like the image of a shepherd, especially because the Bible says that a shepherd must be willing to lay down his life for his sheep.

A shepherd is an overseer of those who are under him and one who is responsible for their well-being. Honestly, I look at police supervisors and administrators as shepherds, because if you are a boss in a police department, one of your major charges is to care for the well-being of your subordinates.

From a spiritual point of view, God takes a great interest in those who are responsible for caring for the needs of others. St. Paul knew what it meant to be tasked with overseeing the care of subordinates when he wrote, "Besides everything else, I face daily the pressure of my concern for all the churches. Who is weak, and I do not feel weak? Who is led into sin, and I do not inwardly burn?" (2 Corinthians 11:28-29). When you cross the path of bosses who care for their subordinates like that, you will not soon forget such individuals.

Someone once said that if you think you are leading and no one is following you, you are merely taking a walk. A leader is more than a person who makes sure that assignments or tasks are accomplished. People who just do that are not leaders, but rather managers. Managers manage people and projects. Although that is part of the job description of a leader, it is not enough. I have unfortunately run across a lot of managers in police work. Some may even be considered taskmasters, but no one is following them—or at least not following them with respect. Many in supervision know how to herd people, but they don't know how to lead them. You see, a leader teaches and inspires others to not only accomplish a task, but also moves them beyond their own expectations.

I have worked for bosses who could rarely be satisfied and who seldom offered praise. That's what taskmasters do, not leaders. Then again, I have worked for some true leaders such as Inspector John Martin who commanded the Midtown South Precinct in midtown Manhattan. The Midtown South Precinct is the largest and busiest precinct in the world with over 550 police officers assigned to that one command. Inspector Martin could be tough—but he also readily exhibited his appreciation for officers and supervisors who worked hard and did their job well. He regularly visited with the officers at roll calls and out on patrol in order to get to know those who were assigned to his command. He spent quality time explaining his vision, goals, and objectives with his supervisors. As one of his plainclothes supervisors, I often sat and listened as he shared with me his years of experience and wisdom. He took great joy in helping shape his subordinates. This was a commander who had 550 police officers and dozens of civilian personnel under his command, and yet he still made the time to connect. I know chiefs of departments with fewer than 100 officers in their agency who remain locked up in their offices, staring at a computer screen, and never connecting with anyone but city council members.

Simply having enough time in service to take a promotion exam, passing that test, and overcoming other promotion requirements, does not necessarily make you a leader. It merely gets you promoted to a leadership position—the hard work follows the minute after the promotion ceremony.

Supervision at 3,000 Feet

It has been my experience that leaders should always look at the large picture rather than merely focusing on the narrow area within the scope of their responsibility. Managers and three-striped police officers who are not leaders come to work, do their assigned tasks like that of a trained canine dog, clock out, and go home until their next shift. Real leaders always take what I call a "3,000 feet view" of the department. I remember when I was a paratrooper and my unit gathered on the tarmac of an airstrip to put on our equipment, get checked by a jumpmaster, and wait to board a C-130 for our transportation and jump. Usually, there were delays and long waits before the aircraft was ready to receive us. During the wait we would either walk awkwardly around with all of our equipment, weapons and main and reserve parachutes strapped to us, or just sit down on the blacktop and stare. As I sat there I would look around while thinking about the jump or our mission. I would notice almost every pebble, every crack in the pavement, and every detail of my immediate surroundings. However, when I stood in the open door of that C-130 traveling 120 miles per hour at 3,000 feet, I was able to see the wide panoramic span of the terrain below. I could see farm houses, fields, dirt roads, tree lines, power lines, and waterways—all because I was high enough to see the bigger picture. The same is true for 3,000 feet leadership.

The effective police leader always looks at the bigger picture and attempts to see how each component of the department compliments or affects the other. To merely focus on the narrow scope of your responsibility stymies your ability to offer great and effective contributions that would enhance the effectiveness of the overall operation of

141

the department. When you can learn how to lead from 3,000 feet, you will gain the respect of your superiors and subordinates alike.

Narrow vision leads to self-centeredness, a complaining spirit, and ineffectiveness. Once you understand what the chief and others who are up the line in the chain of command have to deal with on a regular basis, you will then gain a greater appreciation for what they do and find ways to assist in the department's operation, rather than always complaining about the brass upstairs or down the hall.

St. Paul even had a word for police officers as centurions to make every effort to please your commanding officer (2 Timothy 2:4). Remember, respect and caring goes both ways—not just from the top down.

One of the greatest problems facing police departments today has very little to do with criminal activity, but rather with low morale and a lack of unity within the agency. The police chief, commissioner, commander, or sheriff is directly responsible for the morale of the department. That overall responsibility cannot be relegated to anyone else. As I shared earlier, I have personally worked for bosses who kept themselves locked up in their offices like ostriches with their heads buried in the sand and completely out of touch with what was going on regarding morale in their department. They either assumed everything was okay or frankly didn't care enough, just as long as the numbers fell in place at the end of the month for reporting purposes to the city's hierarchy.

When the appearance of a lack of concern about the well-being of the troops works its way down and penetrates the rank and file, there is usually a breakdown in unity and morale that directly affects the quality of service rendered to the public. But let me also point out that some departments can breed complaining and whining, spoiled brats who have to be consistently placated like unruly kids in crowded supermarket checkout lines. I have seen police officers given one perk and benefit after the other, only to come back and say, "What have you done for me lately?" That's not acceptable, either.

A police department is a para-military body with rules and regulations, rank structure, disciplinary policies, direct orders, and a chain of command. Therefore, a commander or supervisor should be a boss and not merely everybody's best friend. I would occasionally inherit a sergeant who I called a "Three-striped Patrolman," who never really made the transition from police officer to boss. This type of supervisor may be loved by the troops, but rarely respected, and there *is* a difference.

I presently volunteer as a chaplain with a police department in Western Connecticut, not far from where I pastor a church. I am privileged and blessed to be a close acquaintance with a detective sergeant, Jim Wright, who also happens to be an active member of the congregation I pastor. It is clear that Jim honors God in everything he does. God, being reciprocal, honors Jim in return. As a result of Jim not forgetting his first love of the Lord, his leadership is honored, and this former ten-year Navy Seabee veteran has the respect of his family, his department, and the people in the community he serves. Honoring God may not bring you a framed certificate or plaque to place on your office wall, but it will provide you with an immovable foundation from which to base your life and role as a police officer and supervisor. When you honor God you will not compromise on your values. When God takes first place in your life, the way you see and treat others takes on a whole different perspective. Jesus said in Matthew 22:37-38, "Love the Lord your God with all your heart and with all your soul and with all your mind."

Police work exposes you to a lot of negativity. That negativity can have an affect on you that can easily cause you to do things that you know you should not do. This is why I believe it is so important to have a relationship with God. St. Paul said that God would "tell you where to go and what to do, and then you won't always be doing the wrong things your evil nature wants you to. For we naturally love to do evil things that are just the opposite from the things that the Holy Spirit tells us to do; and the good things we want to do when the Spirit has his way with us are just the opposite of our natural desires. These two forces within us are constantly fighting each other to win control over us, and our wishes are never free from their pressures" (Galatians 5:16-17, TLB).

There will always be that struggle for your conscience. And there is no place where that struggle is stronger than police work.

Generation X Cops: Are They a Problem or an Opportunity?

Not long ago, a patrol sergeant drove up to my office at the church to have a chat with me. He was frustrated and said, "Pastor Chuck, I don't know what to do with these young guys. This Generation X

143

is all about them. They isolate themselves. They won't do anything extra unless they are compensated, and even then they want to leave the station the minute their shift is over. You want to know why? They want to rush home to go on the internet to play video games competing against the rest of their geek friends out there in cyberspace! You tell them to do something, they ask, 'Why?' Why? Because I have the damn chevrons on my sleeve, that's why!"

This sergeant was getting all worked up over his experiences supervising the new generation of cops known as GenXers (born between 1965-1981). Many of the supervisors and upper management of the department are Baby Boomers (born between 1946 and 1964) who were students of the Veterans (born between 1922-1945). The Veterans taught that if you work hard and keep your nose clean; everything turns out alright. They also taught that when someone who is in charge gives you an order, the only response is "Yes, Sir."

The biggest complaints I hear from police supervisors, an echo of what that sergeant said to me in my office, is that GenXers do not appear to be committed to the department, are not willing to pay their dues, and have no respect for authority. Of course, those are sweeping charges that cannot be pinned on an entire generation.

I want to encourage older officers to hold out hope for the next generation. There is a wonderful opportunity for you to help the up-and-coming police officers to carry on the great tradition of your department. Remember, they may be different than you and perhaps hold some different values than you do—but they can do the job and do it well. They will comprise the workforce for the next 20 to 30 years. They are the future.

Unlike the Baby Boomer generation that poured enormous numbers into the workforce, we are competing for an ever shrinking labor pool with this new generation. Why do you think there are so many "help-wanted" signs everywhere and the military services are offering hundreds of thousands of dollars as re-up bonuses? When I took my oath with the NYPD, I knew that I would finish my police career there. That is not the outlook of most police officers today—though larger departments tend to keep their officers due to the vast opportunities that are available for promotion and new assignments.

My fellow Baby Boomers hold a whole different set of norms than do GenXers. Discipline was not only expected, it was inevitable. It was true that if the local patrolman put a nightstick to your backside and brought you home, your father would give you a second beating just for good measure. We were taught never to call adults by their first names. The teachers and deans of the public schools I attended could grab you by the small of you neck if you were out of order. Those days are over.

Baby Boomers had definable heroes like John Wayne, President John F. Kennedy Jr., Mickey Mantle, and Mr. Shuller, my Boy Scout leader. Television consisted of *Leave It to Beaver*, *Davy Crockett*, *Sky King*, *Roy Rodgers*, and *Zorro*. But the mid-1960s brought a whole new set of values. The catchphrase for that era was "challenge authority."

Looking back on it, some of that societal shake-up needed to occur. Although most of us who grew up in the 1950s and early 1960s have fond memories of the good old days, Mrs. Rosa Parks still had to sit in the back of the bus. There were separate water fountains and lunch counters for the races. Dr. Martin Luther King Jr. provoked our culture to seek justice over prejudice. That kind of challenge needed to be issued.

In the midst of that agonizing era, however, there were other aspects of the culture that bred contempt for parents, the Church, and virtually all other aspects of authority. The "free love" philosophy and an extensive drug culture delivered a one-two punch to our nation.

Many of these up-and-coming officers are children of that generation. They commonly witnessed the divorce of their parents. They were often left home alone as latchkey kids while their parent or parents sought careers and spent long hours away from the family. We have to be slow to point our fingers at one generation, when our own has so much to answer for.

GenXers were firsthand witnesses of what workaholics looked like and how that kind of lifestyle does not bring happiness. They do not wish to travel down that same path. They are not as readily excited about immersing themselves in a career for the purpose of identity or happiness. Some of them were left to fend for themselves as children and so now they tend to be much more autonomous. Team-building Baby Boomer supervisors and administrators find this autonomous attitude frustrating. They often interpret such display of behavior as being disloyal.

Some GenXers have good reason to be irritated with older generations. Boomers were able to buy their homes in the suburbs at affordable prices—while Xers can barely afford to pay the rent for an apartment. Those over 60 will get back about $200 for every $100 they put into Social Security, yet Xers will lose more than $100 for every $450 they contribute. Xers see the workplace differently than the previous generation—and most experts believe that Baby Boomers will not be able to convert them to their way of thinking.

I have been told by several GenX cops that the job is important but it isn't their life. They enjoy other interests outside the job—even if it is playing competitive video games. Supervisors and administrators will have to identify and understand GenX personality characteristics if they wish to communicate with them and motivate these young officers.

Claire Raines, author of *Beyond Generation X*, provides a list of things that GenXers seek from their supervisors. These requests are:[40]

Appreciate us. (*Show you care.*)

Be flexible. (*Let us have a life beyond work.*)

Create a team. (*Give us the family we never had.*)

Develop us. (*Help us to increase our skills.*)

Involve us. (*Ask our opinions.*)

Lighten up. (*Remember, it's not brain surgery.*)

Walk your talk. (*Practice what you preach.*)

I realize that police departments are paramilitary organizations where there is rank and organizational structure; where orders must be followed with consequences if they are not. However, after reviewing the above list I do not believe any one request is unreasonable for a supervisor to meet. Supervisors should show appreciation to their subordinates. Rigidity in leadership is not a good characteristic. Building a team effort as opposed to "do it because I said to do it" philosophy is a positive way to go in supervisory style. Developing subordinates is a given if you are an effective leader. Not being so uptight will relax your subordinates and cause them to seek out your advice and direction. Walking your talk is a must. A leader cannot give the impression of "do as I say and not as I do."

GenX cops are looking for validation. They want their opinions respected and not necessarily implemented all the time. The statement by a supervisor, "That's just the way it is," is hard for GenXers to swallow—even if that is the reality.

I had a young twenty-something-year-old officer say to me, "Sometimes I feel as if this department wants robots that they can program rather than having real living, breathing, thinking human beings." Supervisors need to be secure enough to tap into the GenXer's creativity, technical skills, and ability to think outside the box without feeling threatened. The same young officer I just mentioned praised one of his sergeants explaining how the sergeant, a Baby Boomer in his early fifties, accepted the younger officers for their uniqueness. He said, "Sarge has a real personality that connects with us young guys. He takes the time to explain assignments and why new department policies are implemented. We can ask questions during briefing without feeling like a jerk. When he's the shift supervisor, I believe we are the most productive and happiest."

It didn't cost that sergeant any more time during roll call than his fellow sergeants. It just required going the extra mile to connect with the younger officers. You can do it, but it will necessitate a change in the way you were raised and in the way you may have been taught to supervise.

I met with the sergeant mentioned by the younger officer to discover why he was so successful with his troops. I discovered that he took an honest interest in his people. He makes it his business to learn about the lives of his subordinates, where they grew up, what things they like to do, stories about their families, and what their future goals are. When opportunities present themselves, he tells them about his life. In other words, he makes a connection—he's a real person to his young subordinates and it does not diminish the respect they have for him or his rank. In fact, it has increased it. The sergeant said to me, "There's a thin line between giving them the impression that you're their friend and that you are a real person and still their boss. I don't want to be their friend—I'm their boss—but I do want to connect with them."

Fifteen years after I left the NYPD, I returned with three ranking administrators of a department in South Florida to tour and learn some of the operational dynamics and successes New York was experiencing. At the time a former young officer who worked for me had risen to the rank of deputy commissioner and we were visiting him in his office in police headquarters. While we were there another former young officer who worked for me when I was the plainclothes supervisor in Midtown South walked in. He now had the rank of deputy inspector. I was so proud of both of these men.

Jimmy was the commanding officer of the 5th Precinct in

Chinatown. He greeted me with a big hug and a wide grin from ear to ear. It was as if he was one of my sons. I just beamed with pride over his accomplishments after I left the job. Then he said something that really stuck with me. He said, "I'll never forget when you gave me a note of encouragement with a pair of chevrons attached to it. You inspired me to study and remain positive. And look where I am today—I'm a deputy inspector. I still have that note and stripes somewhere in my house." I had completely forgotten that I had done that. But I always tried to inspire and encourage the men and women whom I was charged with the responsibility to lead.

TWENTY ONE

Making Peace with God

A s a police officer, you know how lost and broken our world really is. You witness its corruption on a daily basis while on patrol. Do you remember the homeless man who was set on fire in the subway? And how my partner, Chuck Conners, asked me, "How can one human being do that to another human being?" Well the answer is, and has always been, that we live in a fallen world. The real question remaining to be answered is, Do we have to continue, as individuals, to live in a fallen condition? The answer is no.

Inside every one of us is a hunger that only God can satisfy. One of the early church fathers once wrote, "You have made us for yourself, and the heart of man is restless until it finds rest in you, O Lord." Without a relationship with God, there is a missing part in the overall puzzle of our lives. Jesus Christ is the only one who can make us whole. We hunger for peace, to be made complete, yet too often we ignore the only one who can fulfill that craving. Jesus said, "I am the bread of life. He who comes to me will never go hungry, and he who believes in me will never be thirsty" (John 6:35).

When I stood on that hallowed ground of Ground Zero, I witnessed police officers and firefighters who were very much aware of the pain and struggle in their lives. The raw edges of that pain cut deep into their very souls. Everything that once appeared to be important fell away—the car, the baseball stats, the upcoming vacation. There were so many officers who were open to finally hearing the truth that hope among the devastation could only be found in Christ. That tragedy on September 11, 2001 dramatically brought them face-to-face with the awareness that there was a missing part to their lives.

Let me point out that you cannot earn your way into heaven. Salvation, which means being set free from the consequences of sin (eternal death), and experiencing peace with God and the assurance that we can live now and forever with him,[41] is not purchased by good

149

works or deeds. There are many who believe that their acts of kindness or goodness will win them a place in heaven; that is simply untrue. The Bible says, "He saved us, not because of righteous things we had done, but because of his mercy. He saved us through the washing of rebirth and renewal by the Holy Spirit, whom he poured out on us generously through Jesus Christ our Savior, so that, having been justified by his grace, we might become heirs having the hope of eternal life" (Titus 3:5-7).

An equally dangerous assumption is that everyone is saved regardless of what they believe or do not believe, because God is a big, loving God who wouldn't punish anyone. It is true that God is big and loving. However, he loves us so much he wants what earthly parents want—to make sure we, as his children, do what is right and live a life of purity. It is very tempting to believe that everyone is going to heaven. Unfortunately, that is one of the enemy's most seductive deceptions. I have often heard people say, "We all serve the same God." Although it sounds very warm and comfortable, it is not true. There are gods being served in the world that have nothing to do with the God of the Old and New Testaments, nothing to do with the God of Abraham, Isaac, and Jacob. The many gods of Hinduism, Allah, Buddha, and Hari Krishna are not the same as the God of the Bible and we should not be forced into a position of political correctness to confess that. This is why Jesus said, "I am the way and the truth and the life. No one comes to the Father except through me" (John 14:6). As cops usually tell others, "What part of that statement do you not understand?"

God's Grace

Grace is defined as "unmerited favor," which means you cannot earn it. So when you hear the wonderful hymn, "Amazing Grace," it is truly amazing how God can be so gracious without us having to do a thing. It is through God's unconditional love and grace for you that he provided a way for you to be spared from the consequences of your sins—spiritual death and eternal separation from God. Let's face it, you spend every day looking for those who break the law. Right? And what happens to lawbreakers? They are arrested, tried, convicted, and sentenced. There are consequences for their misdeeds. The same is true for those of us who sin.

The Bible makes it clear that we are all in the same boat: "For all have sinned and fall short of the glory of God, and are justified freely by his grace through the redemption that came by Christ Jesus" (Romans 3:23-24).

No one seems to be exempt from the need of God's grace in order to be justified and redeemed through Jesus. It is only through God's love, grace, and mercy that we can be saved. I am sure you have heard John 3:16: "For God so loved the world that he gave his one and only son, that whoever believes in him shall not perish but have eternal life." Just rephrase that sentence by making it personal: "For God so loved *me* that he gave his one and only son, that if *I* believe in him *I* shall not perish but have eternal life." That is exactly what God offers. His grace is sufficient because that is his end of the deal. But it requires a response from you which the Bible calls "faith."

Faith

We've all heard a lot about faith, but what does it mean? Well, faith means "belief, to believe in, to commit, or trust in." When I was in the Army Airborne, the Air Force would fly my unit up to 3,000 feet and politely ask us to leave their aircraft. This required real faith. I had to have faith in the big, burly jump master standing near the exit door telling us to "Go!" I had to possess enough faith in his ability to select a good DZ (drop zone) that was free of high tension wires, water, and trees. I also had to possess faith in someone I didn't even know—the rigger back on the ground who packed my parachute. Oh, he signed off on the chute he packed, but that wouldn't have done me a whole lot of good if I didn't have a canopy over my head five seconds after leaving a perfectly good C-130 aircraft. To have faith means to believe in someone with a *full measure of trust*—like the big, burly jump master and rigger.

More important than the equipment needed to survive parachuting is having a faith that believes that what God says in the Bible is true and then acting appropriately on those words. I could have had all the faith in the world in my jump master and rigger and never left the aircraft. But my faith in action took form when I jumped out the door into thin air.

Faith in action

As I mentioned in an earlier part of this book, the number one priority code for an NYPD police officer is a code 10-13, "Officer in need of help—Officer in trouble." There is not a single code listed that takes a precedent over a code 10-13. It means that a police officer somewhere out there is calling for help, and nothing is spared to get him or her that help. Well, the Bible says, "Everyone who calls on the name of the Lord will be saved" (Romans 10:13). That is a divine code 10-13.

We know that not a single person who ever walked on the face of this earth was without sin, except Jesus himself. Sin, which means missing the mark of what God intends for our lives, hinders a relationship with God. It is Satan's desire to keep you in a place that is out of fellowship with God. But Jesus has authority and dominion over Satan.

So how do we clear up that sin in our lives? St. John said, "If we confess our sins, [God] is faithful and just and will forgive us our sins and purify us from all unrighteousness" (1 John 1:9). I know the enemy would want you to believe that you've committed things that just could not be forgiven. You may be thinking that God could never forgive you for what you had done in the past. Look, if God said it, he meant it. You can find forgiveness. You don't have to walk on burning coals or crawl up cathedral steps on your hands and knees. You may be saying, "But you don't understand where I've been and what I have done." Even if I don't, God does, and he loves you so much that he gave his only son as a sacrifice to cover and remove your sins. Even if you were the only person on earth, Jesus would have still gone to the cross just for you.

Are you willing to repent and have a change of mind and heart about the way you are living your life? By now you may realize that materialism doesn't bring lasting peace and happiness. A new car or truck brings temporary happiness. There is the new smell of the interior of the car and a body without a scratch. You wash and wax it on a regular basis, park it in places where no one could ding it with the careless opening of their car door. But we all know that after a while it just becomes a car or a truck. We appreciate it for what it provides, but it doesn't provide lasting happiness and peace, does it?

Perhaps you strived so hard for a promotion and you just knew that it would bring you permanent happiness, only to discover that although you appreciate the job and its benefits, in and of itself it does not provide what you are truly striving for. The only way you are going to find lasting joy and a complete change of life is by seeking it from the only One who can provide it—Jesus. So if you are tired of doing things the same old way over and over again and want to change your life, just consider repeating the following prayer from your heart:

Dear Heavenly Father,
I know that I am a sinner and I need your forgiveness. Jesus, I believe that you died for my sins. I want to turn from my sins. I now invite you to come into my heart and life. I accept your loving forgiveness. I ask for your help in leading a new, changed life. From this day forward, with your help, I will honor you. I place all of my trust in you and make you the Lord of my life and receive you as Savior of my life. Thank you for your grace and for my salvation. From this day forward, with your help, I will follow you all the days of my life. In Jesus' name, amen.

If you have said this prayer and truly made a decision to receive Christ into your life and heart, you have every reason to believe he has forgiven you and has come into your heart. Thank him for his forgiveness.

I now encourage you to prayerfully seek a local church to attend. You have taken the first step, now you need to get into a good Christian fellowship, a church, that will assist you in growing as a new believer and that provides a clear teaching of the Bible. If you are not sure which church to attend, perhaps you can ask your chaplain.

Closing Thoughts

Why did I write this book in the first place? It is a legitimate question for anyone to ask who is expected to take his or her precious time and resources to read it. I had to ask this question of myself before I penned the first sentence.

As I grew older, a realization came over me that my story is part of a long illustrious policing history in the greatest city in the world, dating back to the Dutch in the seventeenth century. Granted, there are literally millions of stories that help make up the complete history of the New York City Police Department, many of which have never been told and will never be known, apart from those who lived it. Nevertheless, I wanted to somehow share some of my experiences that might be of some interest and help to others who still do the job.

I am just a common man who grew up in Brooklyn and a former New York City cop who was given the opportunity to have worked alongside heroes. The real heroes have their names etched in the granite wall of fallen officers, located in Battery Park and on the National Monument in Washington, D.C. I especially remember my good and faithful friend, Police Officer Cecil Frank Sledge, who personally witnessed Christ to me before I ever came to know Him as my personal savior. I pay tribute and honor to Officer Bobby Biladeaux, who I knew to be a living hero while he patrolled the mean streets of New York and as a fallen hero who unfortunately died in my arms.

I am certain that someone in the NYPD is now wearing the badge I wore while I was an active cop. And I am certain that badge number 25812 is being worn with the same pride and commitment to duty as I had over the years.

This book is written in honor of God and in honor of all those who have served, those who are still serving, and those yet to raise their right hand and take the oath of office as a law enforcement officer.

APPENDIX A
"The Badge"
An Open Letter to the Law Enforcement Community from an FBI Director

A law enforcement officer's badge is a symbol of public faith. His complex and heavy responsibilities represent a public trust. Whenever an officer breaks this faith or violates this trust, the collective image of law enforcement suffers.

In recent years, law enforcement has made great progress. Equipment and facilities have improved. Significant and far reaching scientific advances have been made. However, all these achievements are meaningless unless every officer is morally committed to the ethics of professional police service.

Under prevailing conditions, this commitment requires perseverance of the highest order. Daily, in many areas, the law enforcement officer is the principal target of abuse from mobs and dissident groups. He is subjected to personal insults and physical attacks, and increasingly, he is falsely accused of brutality by persons who seek alibis and excuses for their criminal acts. Even so, his conduct must be above reproach. He must exercise self-restraint and remain calm and courageous, never deviating from this code of ethics.

There is no substitute for high principles. Where ideals or justice are concerned, there can be no laxity. The ethics of an enforcement agency are no better than the ethics of its weakest officer. Honesty and integrity must ride in every cruiser, walk every beat, influence every command, and answer every roll call. Good ethics must be in evidence whenever and wherever duty calls, every minute of every day.

Compromise, personal feelings, animosities, and prejudices have no place in professional police service. Free handouts, cut-rate prices, gratuities, and preferential treatment are luxuries an officer cannot accept if he is to keep his professional dignity. These seemingly insignificant matters destroy an officer's objectivity and affect his official actions. All officers must strive to erase the ugly public image of the policeman without character. Absolute integrity is the only answer.

As we enter the New Year, let us make certain that the ethics which our work reflects, the ethics which we pledge to uphold, and the ethics in which we believe are one and the same—ethics of good police service.

APPENDIX B
25 Most Stressful Law Enforcement
Critical Life Events[42]

- Violent death of a partner in the line of duty
- Dismissal
- Taking a life in the line of duty
- Shooting someone in the line of duty
- Suicide of an officer who is close friend
- Violent death of another officer in the line of duty
- Murder committed by a police officer
- Duty-related violent injury (shooting)
- Violent job-related injury to another
- Being suspended
- Being passed over for promotion
- Answering a call to a scene involving violent non-accidental death of a child
- Receiving an assignment away from family for a long period of time
- Personal involvement in a shooting incident
- Reduction in pay
- Observing an act of police corruption
- Accepting a bribe
- Participating in an act of police corruption
- Participating in a hostage situation resulting from aborted criminal action
- Responding to a scene involving the accidental death of a child
- Promotion of inexperienced/incompetent coworker over officer
- Experiencing an Internal Affairs investigation
- Barricading a suspect
- Hostage situation resulting from a domestic disturbance

APPENDIX C
Recognizing Problems: Behavioral Checklist[43]

Use this checklist when you are concerned about an officer's declining performance or behavior problems. Be especially aware of *changes* in an officer's job performance, time and attendance, and behavior.

Officer's appearance:
☐ Sloppy/Unkempt
☐ Inappropriate clothing
☐ Poor hygiene
☐ Appearance different; tired

Officer's mood:
☐ Irritable with others
☐ Mood swings, high and low
☐ Temper outbursts
☐ Suspicious, overly paranoid
☐ Anxious, nervous
☐ Extremely sensitive
☐ Confused
☐ Preoccupied with illness, death

Officer's behavior:
☐ Complains of brutality
☐ Unduly talkative, constant complaining
☐ Physically intimidating
☐ Frequently argumentative
☐ Exaggerated self importance
☐ Outbursts, overly emotional
☐ Rigid–unable to change

Time and attendance:
☐ Excessive sick leave
☐ Frequent use of unscheduled vacation time
☐ Calls in for the first hour often
☐ Unauthorized leave

☐ Repeated absences following a pattern
☐ Takes the last hour(s) off
☐ Peculiar and improbable excuses for absence
☐ Frequent unscheduled short-term absences with or without medical explanations
☐ High absenteeism rate for colds, flu, etc.
☐ Off-beat more than job requires

Accidents:
☐ Accidents on job
☐ Accidents off the job
☐ Injuries on the job

Work patterns:
☐ Requires more effort for work assignments
☐ Complaints and negative comments from other officers
☐ Requires more time for work assignments
☐ Verbally abusive
☐ Has difficulty recalling instructions
☐ Drinks on duty; smells of alcohol
☐ Attitude problems
☐ Deliberately places himself in danger
☐ Disinterest in work
☐ Careless, reckless behavior
☐ Receives citizens' complaints
☐ Drinks excessively off duty
☐ Preoccupied, absentminded
☐ Argues with supervisor
☐ Overly aggressive on the street
☐ Overexerts during runs
☐ Provokes citizens to violence

Relationships on the job:
☐ Involved in "love triangles"
☐ Complaints from other officers
☐ Has reputation for promiscuity
☐ Other officers request not to work with officer

Family relationships/person problems:
☐ Spouse/significant other calls supervisor complains about officer's behavior
☐ Illness in officer's family
☐ Divorce/separation
☐ Financial problems
☐ Death of family member
☐ Duty-related lawsuit

Critical incidents
☐ Military Veteran
☐ Suspension
☐ Has used deadly force
☐ Put on "non-contact" status
☐ Partner/friend has committed suicide

APPENDIX D
Distinguishing Characteristics of
Police Burn-out[44]

The burn-out pattern is a familiar experience in every police department. It begins with an officer who is gung-ho to be the best cop on the force. Eventually the frustration of police work begins to wear him down. He begins to resent his superiors and the establishment "downtown." He begins to abuse alcohol or other chemicals, including prescriptions. His home life, already disrupted by his odd working hours, deteriorates further. On the job, he stops taking the initiative, complaining that the courts will only throw his cases out anyway.

He answers as few calls as possible, and those he does answer, he deals with in a lackadaisical way. Soon reports of misconduct begin filtering back to his supervisors. If the stress and bad attitudes are not dealt with, they will lead to a condition associated with tired and frustrated officers: burn-out.

"Burn-out" has many definitions, each containing the same traits. Some of them are:
- Emotional exhaustion
- Depersonalization
- Sleep depravation or excessive sleep
- Decreased or increased appetite
- Decreased sexual functioning or enjoyment of sex
- Reduced personal accomplishments
- Low morale
- Ceases to be a visionary
- Loss of physical, emotional, and mental energy
- Loss of direction
- Feelings of helplessness
- Feelings of hopelessness
- Development of a negative attitude toward work
- Development of unacceptable attitudes toward others and self
- Irritable
- Decreased effectiveness and capability
- Worn out striving for unrealistic expectations imposed by self or others

- Worn out by doing what has to be done
- Inability to cope adequately with stress of work and personal life
- A loss of will
- Accumulation of intense negative feelings
- Withdrawal from important situations
- Anxiety gives way to depression
- Depression gives way to despair
- Uses inadequate coping mechanisms to reduce stress
- Loss of humor
- Loss of satisfaction
- Decreased ability to concentrate
- Employment becomes "just a paycheck"
- Circumstances produce shut-down because of high pressure demands

I. The Anatomy of Burn-out

Burn-out is the disease of the over-committed. It comes as a result of chronic stress: disappointment leading to loss of faith in people; failure to show real self; is called only when needed; will almost never say no; unfulfilled desire to be treated like an ordinary person; time pressures and deadlines; boredom or lack of meaning in performing the job; open communication blocked; open show of emotions blocked.

II. Results of Burn-out

Anger: Mad at organization, self, and public.

Judgmental: Believes everyone is a hypocrite.

Vices: Abuses drinking, sex, tobacco, and chemical uses.

Denial: Ignores problems.

Reclusive: Associates only with other officers.

Eating: Binges. Diets. Uses food to console self.

Fault Finding: Has judgmental attitude. Complains.

Illness: Develops headaches or major illness. Becomes accident-prone.

Indulging: Stays up late, sleeps in. Wastes time. Buys on impulse.

Passivity: Hopes problems get better. Procrastinates. Waits for luck to change.

Revenge: Criticizes, gets even, is sarcastic, and talks mean.

Stubbornness: Is rigid and demanding. Refuses to acknowledge wrongs.

Tantrums: Yells, mopes, pouts, swears, or drives recklessly.

Withdrawal: Avoids situations. Skips work. Keeps feelings to self.

Worrying: Frets over things. Imagines the worst scenarios.

Loss: Loses productivity.

III. Providing Help for Victims of Burn-out

Teach the following in the academy, in-service training, and in daily contact:

- Tell them to not take themselves too seriously.
- Tell them not to be a cop at home.
- Tell them to have more than only cops for friends.
- Help them dump their emotional trash.
- Be "real" to them.
- Suggest other activities for them.
- Run interference for them whenever possible.
- Provide helpful activity ideas: i.e., exercise, rest, vacations, etc.
- Encourage them to take time out, off duty.
- Give positive directions for living.
- Let them know that authority comes from servanthood—presumed, assumed, or assigned.
- Assign a positive role model supervisor.
- Respond to the "red flags"—early warning signs.
- Help them concentrate efforts on "real work" and not "nothing work."
- Teach self-calming techniques following stressful situations.
- Teach them to occasionally say "no" to extra activities.

Burn-out Summary:

It is a sign of strength to be able to admit you have a problem, whether or not it is recognized as burn-out.

Burned-out individuals should be challenged. If not challenged, cliques of burn-outs form and eventually dominate the department. This usually carries the label of "low morale." The more burned-out a person becomes without the department doing anything about it, the more that person controls the process. Supervision tends to give in more easily to burned-out officers, even to isolate themselves from them, for a very human reason. We don't like to have people around us who are sick. We avoid dealing with them when we can. As a result, many burn-outs are often assigned to the same detail, precinct, or district.

Burn-out can start at either the bottom of the chain and flow uphill or at the top and flow downhill. If a burn-out program is going to be successful, it has to belong to the department with the full support from top management.

Burn-out should be recognized as a temporary, not a permanent character disorder. Just as a patrol car without brakes must be repaired; an overwrought officer deserves no less.

APPENDIX E
Suicide Intervention for Peers[45]

Level of Suicidal Threat	Level of Reaction
Personal Crisis	• Listen carefully • Suggest alternatives • Suggest professional help • Officer friendship, support, guidance
Suspicion of suicidal thinking	• Ask direct questions about suicidal potential • Listen carefully • Suggest alternatives • Suggest professional help • Offer friendship, support, guidance
Change in normal behavior	• Ask direct questions about suicidal potential
Deepening depression	• Listen carefully
Deteriorating performance	• Validate feelings
Angry outbursts	• Ask about the person's history (others who have committed suicide, etc.)
Sleep disturbances	• Urge change
Unclear thinking	• Urge professional help
Withdrawal	• Ask about possibly helpful resources
Subtle or clear statements about suicide	• Assist in finding and using resources

	• Make direct referrals, if possible • Reduce stress for the person • Monitor the situation
Threat of suicide when on or off duty	• Remove the person from work, if necessary
Behavior indicative of imminent suicide	• Direct referral for assistance to clergy, mental health personnel, or other administrative suspension until professional help is obtained. • Contact closest family members if individual does not cooperate
Suicidal act on duty	• Call police • Restrain, if necessary • Assure safety of all unit members • Hospitalize • Mobilize resources • Be prepared to do whatever is necessary to save a life

APPENDIX F
Facts and Fiction Concerning
Suicide[46]

Fiction: People who talk about suicide won't do it!

Fact: It is estimated that about 80 percent of people who take their lives have given signals about their intentions. Suicide threats should always be taken seriously.

Fiction: Mentioning suicide may give the person the idea.

Fact: For a person who is considering suicide, having someone to talk out the idea with can be a powerful prevention. If the person has not thought about suicide, but is obviously anxious or depressed, talking about suicide as a bad option can be a preventative measure. You can assume, though, that most depressed or very anxious people have given some thought to taking their lives.

Fiction: Suicide occurs without warning.

Fact: Suicide is the result of a process that can be traced back, sometimes for years. The suicidal person almost always plans how he will take his life and then gives clues to his intentions.

Fiction: Suicide is the result of a mental illness.

Fact: Although the suicidal person may be unhappy, anxious and upset, not all people who take their lives could be diagnosed as mentally ill.

Fiction: Once people are, suicidal, they are and always will be, beyond help.

Fact: The suicidal crisis is generally of a brief duration and if intervention and therapy occur, the person may never again seriously contemplate suicide. It is true, however, that about ten percent of the people who attempt suicide will eventually take their lives. (Of all who *attempt* suicide, only ten percent complete the act. Of all who *complete* the act, about 45 percent have attempted it previously.)

Fiction: A suicidal person is completely committed to dying.

Fact: The dominant feeling of most suicidal people is ambivalence. They want to die, but also want to live.

Fiction: The very poor or very rich are the most likely to destroy themselves.

Fact: Suicide crosses all socioeconomic boundaries. No one group has a proportionately higher incidence than another.

Fiction: People who are alcoholics do not usually commit suicide.

Fact: There is a high correlation between alcoholism and suicide, with an estimated one of every five alcoholics ending their lives by suicide. Many people who are not alcoholics drink heavily prior to killing themselves.

Fiction: Suicidal people do not seek medical help.

Fact: Several studies have indicated that as many as 75 percent of people who take their lives visited a physician within three months prior to killing themselves.

Fiction: Professionals do not commit suicide.

Fact: There is a high suicide rate among physicians, dentists, pharmacists, and lawyers. (Police officers rank in the top percentile of professionals who take their own lives.)

Fiction: December has the highest suicide rate of any month.

Fact: December is the lowest rate. April and May have the highest rates.

APPENDIX G
Recognizing an Officer with Post Traumatic Stress Disorder (PTSD)

Intrusion—Most officers with PTSD will experience one or more:
- Extreme nightmares
- Extreme paranoia
- Sense of shortened future, impending doom

Avoidance—Most officers with PTSD will experience three or more:
- Loss of interest in sex
- Depression
- Isolation—especially from loved ones
- Increased absenteeism
- Avoids certain previously visited location that were favorites
- Waning activities, sports, and people
- Lack of motivation
- Constantly fatigued
- Loss of faith in God
- Sleeps too much
- Addictions to alcohol, drugs, or sex
- Previously active in work; significant shift to doing little or nothing
- Weak or significant drop in work performance
- Stops exercise and previous self-car (poor hygiene)
- Memory loss
- Disappears for periods of time from home or work

Arousal—Most officers with PTSD will experience three or more:
- Insomnia
- Irritability
- Worse than usual problems with supervisors and/or the public
- Increasingly cynical

- Sudden outbursts of anger, rage, and overreacting to the situation at hand
- Hyper vigilance (paranoia)
- Exaggerated startled response
- Obsessive behavior
- Compulsive behavior
- Overeats: noticeable weight gain
- Anorexia: noticeable weight loss
- More hyperactive

Somatic Problems—Not all victims will experience these symptoms, but at least one is not uncommon:

- Problems urinating
- Frequent headaches
- Chest pains
- Intestinal pain
- Diarrhea, constipation, irritable bowel syndrome, blood in stool
- Frequent belching
- Very high use of antacids

APPENDIX H
PTSD and the Family

The entire family is profoundly affected when any family member experiences psychological trauma and suffers Post Traumatic Stress Disorder (PTSD). Some traumas are directly experienced by only one family member, but other family members may experience shock, fear, anger, and pain in their own unique ways simply because they care about and are connected to the survivor.

Living with an individual who has PTSD does not automatically cause PTSD, but it can produce vicarious or secondary trauma. Whether family members live together or apart, are in contact often or rarely, and feel close or distant emotionally from one another, PTSD affects each member of the family in several ways.

Family members may feel hurt, alienated, frustrated, or discouraged if the person loses interest in family or intimate activities and is easily angered or emotionally isolated and detached. Family members often end up feeling distant or angry toward the person, especially if he or she seems unable to relax without being irritable, tense, anxious, worried, distractible, or controlling, overprotective, and demanding.

Even if the trauma occurred decades ago, survivors may act—and family members may feel—as if the trauma never stops happening. They may feel as if they are living in a war zone or a disaster if the survivor is excessively on-guard, tense, or easily startled or enraged. Family members can find themselves avoiding activities or people and becoming isolated from each other and from friends outside the family. They may feel that they have no one to talk to and that no one can understand.

Family members may find it very difficult to have a cooperative discussion with the person about important plans and decisions for the future, because he or she feels there is no future to look forward to. Because the person has difficulty listening and concentrating without becoming distracted, tense, or anxious, or because he or she becomes angry and overly suspicious toward the family member or toward others (hyper vigilant). They may find it very difficult to discuss personal or family problems because the survivor becomes controlling, demanding, overprotective, or unreasonably anxious and fearful about problems becoming terrible catastrophes.

Family members may become over involved with their children's lives due to feeling lonely and in need of some positive emotional feed-back, or feeling that the partner can't be counted on as a reliable and responsible parent. For the person, this discounting of the partner as a co-parent often is due to hyper vigilance and guilt because of trauma experiences involving children The partner may feel he or she must be the sole caregiver to their children if the survivor is uninvolved with their children (often due to trauma-related anxiety or guilt) or is overly critical, angry, or even abusive.

They may find their sleep disrupted by the trauma survivor's sleep problems (reluctance to sleep at night, restlessness while sleeping, severe nightmares, or episodes of violent sleepwalking. Family members also often find themselves having terrifying nightmares, afraid to go to sleep, or difficulty getting a full and restful night's sleep, as if they are reliving the survivor's trauma in their own feelings and sleep.

Ordinary activities, such as going shopping, going to a movie, or taking a drive in the car may feel like reliving of past trauma when the survivor experiences trauma memories or flashbacks. The person may go into "survival mode" or on "automatic pilot," suddenly and without explanation shutting down emotionally, becoming pressured and angry, or going away abruptly and leaving family members feeling shocked, stranded, helpless, and worried.

Trauma survivors with PTSD often struggle with intense anger or rage, and can have difficulty coping with an impulse to lash out ver-bally or physically—especially if their trauma involved physical abuse or assault, war, domestic, or community violence, or being humiliated, shamed, and betrayed by people they needed to trust. Family members can feel frightened of and betrayed by the survivor, despite feeling love and concern.

Addiction exposes family members to emotional, financial, and (less often, but not uncommonly) domestic violence problems. Survivors experiencing PTSD may seek relief and escape with alco-hol or other drugs, or through addictive behaviors such as gambling, workaholism, overeating, or refusing to eat (bulimia and anorexia). Addictions offer false hope to the survivor by seeming to help for a short time, but then making PTSD's symptoms of fear, anxiety, ten-sion, anger, and emotional numbness far worse. Addictions may be very obvious, such as when binge drinking or daily use of drugs occurs. They may, however involve lighter or less frequent episodes of "using" that are a problem because the survivor is dependent on the habit and can't cope without it.

When suicide is a danger, family members face these unavoidable strains: worry ("How can I know if suicide is going to happen, and what can I do to prevent it?"), guilt ("Am I doing something to make him or her feel so terrible, and should I be doing something to make him or her feel better?"), grief ("I have to prepare myself every day for losing him or her. In many ways I feel and have to live my life as if he or she is already gone."), and anger ("How can he or she be so selfish and uncaring?"). Trauma survivors with PTSD are more prone to contemplate and attempt suicide than similar people who have not experienced trauma or are not suffering from PTSD. For the family there is good and bad news in this respect. The good news is that very few trauma survivors, even those with PTSD, actually attempt or complete suicide. The bad news is that family members with a loved one with PTSD must often deal with the survivor's feelings of sufficient discouragement and depression.

What can families of trauma survivors with PTSD do to care for themselves and for the survivor?

Continue to learn more about PTSD by attending classes, viewing films, or reading books. Encourage—but don't pressure—the survivor to seek counseling from a PTSD specialist. Seek personal, child, couples, or family counseling if troubled by "secondary" trauma reactions such as anxiety, fears, anger, addiction, or problems in school, work, or intimacy. Take classes on stress and anger management, couples communication, or parenting. Stay involved in positive relationships, in productive work and education, and with enjoyable past times. If physical (domestic) violence actually is occurring, family members such as spouses, children, or elders must be protected from harm.

APPENDIX I
Resources

International Association of Chiefs of Police (IACP)
Critical Incident Debriefing Network
Phone: (703) 836-6767 ext. 237

International Critical Incident Stress Foundation (ICISF)
3290 Pine Orchard Lane, Suite 106
Ellicott City, MD 21042
Phone: (410) 750-9600
24-hour Emergency Hotline: (410) 313-2473
Fax: (410) 750-9601
E-mail: info@icisf.org
Website: www.icisf.org

International Conference of Police Chaplains
P.O. Box 5590
Destin, FL 32540
Phone: (850) 654-9736
Website: www.icpc4cops.org

Tears of a Cop Under Pressure
Website: www.tearsofacop.com

TOAC is a helpful "information-only" website dealing with police PTSD and suicide by police officers.

Central Florida Police Stress Unit, Inc.
P.O. Box 149897
Orlando, FL 32814-9897
Phone: (407) 428-1800
24-Hour Emergency Hotline: (407) 428-1800
Website: www.policestressunit.org

The Police Stress Unit provides a confidential response for law enforcement officers with no outside interference from their respective department or agency. Peer-support personnel are on call 24 hours a day, 7 days a week and will respond immediately in emergencies.

Law Enforcement Family, Inc.
1553 SW Belle Avenue
Topeka, KS 66604
Phone: (877) 517-9910
Website: www.lawenforcementfamily.com

Concerns of Police Survivors, Inc (C.O.P.S.)
P.O. Box 3199
846 Old South 5
Camdenton, Missouri 65020-6412
Phone: (573) 346-4911
Website: www.nationalcops.org

C.O.P.S. is a nationwide non-profit 501(c)(3) organization providing resources to assist in the rebuilding of the lives of survivors of law enforcement officers killed in the line of duty as determined by federal government criteria.

Focus on the Family
Colorado Springs, CO 80995
Phone: 1-800-A-Family (232-6459)

Law Enforcement Wellness Association, Inc.
Dedicated to the physical and psychological health of those sworn to serve.
P.O. Box 504
Elmira, OR 97437
Phone: (541) 935-2594
Website: www.cophealth.com

The Law Enforcement Wellness Association has assembled an internationally prominent faculty of professionals dedicated to the overall physical and psychological health of the nation's law enforcement personnel.

The Heavy Badge
Website: www.heavybadge.com

The Heavy Badge sites attempts to explore the effects of stress on law enforcement personnel.

The Officer Down Memorial Page, Inc.
Website: www.odmp.org

The Officer Down Memorial Page lists the most recent line-of-duty deaths, as well as line-of-duty deaths in the past.

Cops Helping Alleviate Policemen's Problems (C.H.A.P.P.s)
Oklahoma City Police Department
701 Colcord
Oklahoma City, OK 73102
Phone: (405) 297-1717
Website: www.members.aol.com/ocpdchapps

APPENDIX J
Avoiding the 10 Fatal Errors

According to The National Law Enforcement Officers Memorial Foundation, there were 153 Law Enforcement Officers killed in the line of duty in 2004. From time to time, especially when we are faced with these harsh realities, it is important we review the Ten Fatal Errors that have killed experienced Lawmen. Perhaps one of them may make a lifesaving difference one day for you!

1. Attitude—If you fail to keep your mind on the job, or you carry personal problems into the field, you will make errors. It can cost your or your fellow officers' lives.

2. Tombstone courage—No one doubts that you have courage. But in any situation where time allows, *wait* for backup. There are few instances where you should try to make a dangerous apprehension alone and unaided.

3. Not enough rest—To do your job you must be alert. Being sleepy or asleep on the job is not only against regulations, but you endanger yourself, the community, and all your fellow officers.

4. Taking a bad position—Never let anyone you are questioning or detaining manipulate you into a position of disadvantage. Always be aware of position. Maintain the advantage. There is no such thing as a routine arrest or stop.

5. Danger signs—As an officer, you should recognize "danger signs." Fast movement and strange cars are warnings that should alert you to watch and approach with caution. Know your community and watch for what looks to be "out of place."

6. Failure to watch the hands of a suspect—Is he reaching for a weapon or getting ready to strike you? How else can a potential killer strike but with his hands?

7. Relaxing too soon—Observe carefully. Are you certain the crisis is over? Don't be quick to relax simply because the immediate and apparent threat has been neutralized.

8. Improper use or no handcuffs—See that the hands that can kill are safely cuffed. Once you have made an arrest, handcuff the prisoner immediately and properly.

9. No search or poor search—There are many places to hide weapons that your failure to search is a crime against fellow officers. Many criminals carry several weapons and are prepared to use them against you.

10. Dirty or inoperative weapon—Are your weapons clean? Will they fire? How about the ammunition? When did you last fire so that you can hit a target in combat conditions? What's the sense of carrying any firearm that may not work when you need it the most?

APPENDIX K
Recommended Reading List

Marriage and Family:

The 10 Commandments of Marriage: The Do's and Don'ts for a Lifelong Covenant. Ed Young. Moody Publishers (2003).

Saving Your Marriage Before It Starts: Seven Questions To Ask Before and After You Marry. Drs. Les & Leslie Parrott. Zondervan (1995).

Making Love Last Forever. Gary Smalley. W Publishing Group (1996).

The Power of a Praying Wife. Stormie Omartian. Harvest House Publishing (1997).

The Power of a Praying Husband. Stormie Omartian. Harvest House Publishing (2001).

Help Me I'm Married. Joyce Meyer. Warner Books. (2000).

The Healthy Marriage Handbook. Broadman & Holman Publishers. (2001).

Every Man's Marriage: Winning the Heart of a Woman. Stephen Arterburn. Waterbrook Press (2001).

Loving Solutions: Overcoming Barriers in Your Marriage. Gary Chapman. Moody Press (1998).

The Five Love Languages: How to Express Heartfelt Commitment to Your Mate. Gary Chapman. Northfield Publishing (1992).

The Other Side of Love: Handling Anger in a Godly Way. Gary Chapman. Moody Press. (1999).

Making Peace with Your Partner: Healing Conflicts in Marriage. H. Norman Wright. Word Publishing (1988).

Fathering Like a Father: Becoming the Dad God Wants You to Be. Kenneth O. Gangel. Baker Books (2003).

Five Signs of a Functional Family. Gary Chapman. Northfield Publishing (1997).

Love Talk: Speak Each Other's Language Like You Never Have Before. Dr. Les & Leslie Parrott. Zondervan (2004).

Boundaries in Marriage. Drs. Henry Cloud & John Townsend. Zondervan (1999).

Strategies for a Successful Marriage: A Study Guide for Men. E. Glenn Wagner. Promise Keepers. NavPress (1994).

Preparing for Marriage: The complete guide to help you discover God's plan for a lifetime of love. David Boehi. Gospel Light Books (1997).

The Truth About Sex. Kay Arthur. Waterbrook Press (2005).

No Time for Sex: Finding the time you need for getting the love you want. David and Claudia Arp. Howard Publishing (2004).

Finding Mr. Right: And how to know when you have. Stephen Arterburn. Thomas Nelson Publishers (2001).

Toward a Growing Marriage: Building the Love Relationship of Your Dreams. Gary Chapman. Moody Press (1996).

The Stepfamily Survival Guide. Natalie Nichols Gillespie. Revell Books (2004).

Winning Your Wife Back before It's too late. Greg Smalley. Thomas Nelson Publishers (1999).

The Power of a Praying Parent. Stormie Omartian. Harvest House (1995).

Every Woman's Battle: Discovering God's plan for sexual and emotional fulfillment. Sharon Ethridge. Waterbrook Press (2003).

Finances:

Debt-Proof Your Marriage: How to Achieve Financial Harmony. Mary Hunt. Revell Books (2003).

Does God Care if I Can't Pay My Bills?: Practical Help and Encouragement for Weathering Your Financial Crisis. Linda K. Taylor. Tyndale House Publishers (1995).

Your Money Counts: The biblical guide to earning, spending, saving, investing, giving and getting out of debt. Howard Dayton. Crown Financial Ministries (1996).

The 33 Laws of Stewardship: Principles for a Life of True Fulfillment. Dave Sutherland. Spire Resources Publishing (2003).

Money Possessions and Eternity. Randy Alcorn. Tyndale House Publishers. (2003).

Good Sense Budget Course: Biblical Financial Principles for Transforming Your Finances and Life. Dick Towner & John Tofilon. Willow Creek Ministries. Zondervan (2004).

Giving & Tithing. Larry Burkett. Moody Press (1991).

Tithing: Discover the Freedom of Biblical Giving. R.T. Kendall. Zondervan (1982).

Nutrition and Health Care:

Greater Health God's Way: 7 Steps to Inner and Outer Beauty. Stormie Omartian. Harvest House Publishers (1996).

Fast Your Way to Health. Lee Bueno-Aguer. Whitaker House (1991).

The Divine Diet: The Secret to Permanent Weight Loss. Carole Lewis. Regal Books (2004).

Lose It For Life: The Total Solution–Spiritual, Emotional, Physical–for Permanent Weight Loss. Integrity Publishers (2004).

Healing and Wholeness:

Experiencing the Father's Embrace: Finding Acceptance in the Arms of a Loving God. Jack Frost. Charisma House (2002).

Lord, Heal My Hurts. Kay Arthur. Multnomah Books (1988).

Total Forgiveness. R.T. Kendall. Charisma House (2002).

Forgive & Forget: Healing the Hurts We Don't Deserve. Lewis B. Smedes. Harper & Row Publishers (1984).

Forgiven and Free. Earl R. Henslin. Thomas Nelson (1991).

Healing of Memories. David A. Seamands. Victor Books (1995).

Healing Your Heart of Painful Emotions. David A. Seamands. Inspirational Press (1993).

Healed Without Scars. David G. Evans. Whitaker House (2004).

Crisis & Trauma Counseling. H. Norman Wright. Regal Books (2003).

Don't Sweat the Small Stuff: And it's All Small Stuff. Richard Carlson. Hyperion Press (1997).

Happiness is a Choice: A Manual on the Symptoms, Causes, and Cures of Depression. Frank B. Minirth. Baker Book House (1978).

In Pursuit of Happiness: Choices That Can Change Your Life. Frank Minirth. Fleming H. Revell Books (2004).

Love Is a Choice: Recovery for codependent relationships. Dr. Robert Hemfelt & Dr. Frank Minirth. Thomas Nelson Publishers (1989).

Angry Men and the Women Who Love Them: Breaking the cycle of physical and emotional abuse. Paul Hegstrom. Beacon Hill Press (2004).

Addiction:

Freedom from Addiction: Breaking the Bondage of Addiction and Finding Freedom in Christ. Neil T. Anderson. Regal Books (1996).

Every Man's Battle: Winning the War on Sexual Temptation One Victory at a Time. Stephen Arterburn. Waterbrook Press (2000).

Celebrate Recovery Materials. Saddle Back Ministries Resource. Zondervan.

Addicted to Love: Understanding Dependencies of the Heart: Romance, Relationships, and Sex. Stephen Arturburn. Vine Books (1991).

Feeding Your Appetites: Take Control of What is Controlling You. Stephen Arterburn. Integrity Publishers (2004).

Suicide:

Police Suicide: Tactics for Prevention. Dell P. Hackett. Charles C. Thomas Publisher, LTD (2003).

Generation X:

Bridging the Boomer Xer Gap. Hank Karp. Davie-Black Publishing (2002).

Beyond Generation X. Claire Raines. Crisp Publications (1997).

Generations At Work: Managing the Clash of Veterans, Boomers, Xers, and Nexters in Your Workplace. Ron Zemke. Amacom (2000).

Leadership:

The 21 Irrefutable Laws of Leadership. John C. Maxwell. Thomas Nelson Publishers (1998).

Developing the Leader Within You. John C. Maxwell. Thomas Nelson Publishers (1993).

Chaplaincy in Law Enforcement: What It Is and How to Do It. Chaplain David W. DeRevere. Charles C. Thomas Publisher (1989).

Heroic Leadership. Chris Lowney. Loyola Press (2003).

Developing the Leaders Around You: How to Help Others Reach Their Full Potential. John C. Maxwell. Thomas Nelson Publishers (1995).

Spiritual Growth and Renewal:

Experiencing God. Henry T. Blackaby. Broadman & Holman

Publishers (1994).

The Purpose Driven Life. Rick Warren. Zondervan Publishers (2002).

New Christian's Handbook: Everything New Believers Need to Know. Max Anders. Thomas Nelson Publishers (1999).

Your Best Life Now: 7 Steps to Living at Your Full Potential. Joel Osteen. Warner Books (2004).

The Life You've Always Wanted: Spiritual Disciplines for Ordinary People. John Ortberg. Zondervan (2002).

Bonds of Iron: Forging Lasting Male Relationships. James Osterhause. Moody Press (1994).

The Life Application Bible. NIV or Living Bible Translations. Tyndale House Publishers (1997).

The Police Officer's Bible. Holman Christian Standard Bible. Holman Bible Publishers (2004).

END NOTES

End Notes

1. For more discussion, see the MacArthur New Testament Commentary, (Moody Press and John MacArthur, Jr., 2004).

2. This code can be found at the website of the International Association of Chiefs of Police IACP Publication, www.theiacp.org, (2005).

3. See *Topical Encyclopedia of Living Quotations*, edited by Sherwood Eliot Wirt, (Minneapolis: Bethany House, 1982) p. 25.

4. Read more daily devotionals in the *Daily Walk Bible* (Atlanta, 1987).

5. For more Mark Twain quotes, visit www.twainquotes.com, (2005).

6. To read the full code, see Scott Snair's, *West Point Leadership Lessons*, (Naperville, IL: Sourcebooks, 2004) p. 32.

7. For the whole "An Open Letter to Police Wives" by Dorothy Fagerstrom, see *Law and Order Magazine*, (Deerfield, IL, May 1971).

8. This quote is from the Rev. Willie Batson's talk at the Vision New England Conference, "Building a Marriage that Lasts," February 8, 2003.

9. For more discussion, see Henry Cloud and John Townsend's book, *Boundaries in Marriage*, (Grand Rapids, MI: Zondervan, 1999) p. 130.

10. For more information, read Stephen R. Covey's *The Seven Habits of Highly Effective People*, (New York: Simon & Schuster, 1989) p. 158.

11. See *The Healthy Marriage Handbook*, edited by Louise A. Ferrebee, (Nashville: Broadman & Holman, 2001) p. 180.

12. These statistics are from marriage coachers and presenters Jerry and Jane Serfass at the Sweetheart Breakfast held at the New Fairfield (CT) United Methodist Church, February 12, 2005.

13. For the complete list, see Tim Kimmel's *Basic Training for a Few Good Men*, (Nashville: Thomas Nelson, 1997) p. 153.

14. See Whit Criswell's article, "First Steps to Happiness and Humility," www.cbmcint.org, (March 2000).

15. See the *United Methodist Hymnal: Book of United Methodist Worship*, (Nashville, TN, 1989): 864.

16. Ibid.

17. See the *United Methodist Hymnal*, p.867

18. For more discussion, see *The Handbook of Bible Application*, edited by Neil S. Wilson, (Wheaton: Tyndale House, 1992) p. 405.

19. See Judith S. Wallerstein, Julia A. Lewis, and Sandra Blakeslee's *The Unexpected Legacy of Divorce*, (New York, 2000): 31, 33-34.

20. See Henry Cloud & John Townsend's *Raising Great Kids*. (Grand Rapids, MI, 1999): 14.

21. For more information on this subject, see Kenneth O. Gangel & Jeffrey S. Gangel's *Fathering like the Father: Becoming the Dad God Wants You to Be*, (Grand Rapids, MI: Baker, 2003) p. 44.

22. See John Maxwell's *Attitude 101*, (Nashville: Thomas Nelson, 2003) p. 4.

23. See Ellen Kirschman's *I Love a Cop*, (New York: The Guilford Press, 1997) p. 19.

24. See David Augsburger's *The New Freedom of Forgiveness*, (Chicago: Moody, 2002) pp. 32-33.

25. This information is from Shannon Hanson's article, "Stress Takes Its Toll on Combat Veterans," *VFW Magazine*, March 2005.

26. See the website for Tears of a Cop: www.tearsofacop.com, (2005).

27. See Hanson article, p.18.

28. See Allen R. Kates' *Cop Shock: Surviving Posttraumatic Stress Disorder*, (Tucson, AZ: Holbrook Street Press, 1999) p. 51.

29. This statistic was taken from the website of the National P.O.L.I.C.E. Suicide Foundation, Inc., www.psf.org, (2005).

30. See Keith W. Strandberg's article, "Suicide in Law Enforcement," *Law Enforcement Technology Magazine*, July 1997.

31. For more information, see Jeffrey Mitchell's book, *Emergency Services Stress*, (New Jersey: Prentice Hall, 1990).

32. For more discussion, see John M. Violanti's book, *Police Suicide: Epidemic in Blue*, (Springfield, IL, 1996): ix.

33. This list is taken from John M. Violanti's book, *Police Suicide: Tactics for Prevention*, (Springfield, IL, 2003): 8.

34. These are all great suggestions taken from the Ministry Department of the Central Florida Police Stress Unit's *The Chaplain's Monthly Messenger*, Volume 1, Number 8, August 1998.

35. See Dr. Paul Quinnett's article, "QPR: Police Suicide Prevention," *FBI Law Enforcement Bulletin*, Volume 6, Number 7, July 1998, p. 19.

36. Ibid., p.20.

37. See Strandberg's article, p. 39.

38. This poem comes from the book *Police Suicide: Tactics for Prevention*, edited by John M. Violanti, (Springfield, IL, 2005): 105.

39. See the ariticle, "The Heart of the Matter," *Law Enforcement News* Vol. XXIV, No. 491. June 15, 1998.

40. For more discussion on this topic, read Claire Raines' book *Beyond Generation X*, (Menlo Park, CA, 1997): 59.

41. See the booklet, *Beginning Your Christian Life*, (Charlotte, NC: Billy Graham Evangelistic Association, 1998) p. 5.

42. This list comes from the Central Florida Police Stress Unit, Inc.

43. Ibid.

44. This information comes from Harold Elliott of the Arlington, Texas Police Department.

45. Ibid.

46. This information was supplied during a seminar by counselor Teresa Tate of the Florida chapter of C.O.P.S.

IF THIS BOOK HAS CHALLENGED OR BLESSED YOU, PLEASE HELP US!

We believe that police officers everywhere will benefit from reading the book you hold in your hands. Our hope is that churches all across America will provide this book for them. Please share this vision with your pastor or missions committee in your local church. Most small towns have no more than five or six police officers. A local church could provide real ministry to their entire police department for a very small investment. We have made special pricing available to those who will help us fulfill this vision:

Single copies are $12 with free shipping.

Five or more copies are $8 each with free shipping.

To order single or multiple copies of *Beyond the Badge*, contact:

**Living Streams Books
Good News Magazine
P.O. Box 132076
The Woodlands, TX 77393-2076**

**Phone: 1-800-487-7784 or 832-813-8327
Email: info@goodnewsmag.org
Website: www.goodnewsmag.org**

Thank you and may God richly bless you!